THE HOLLYWOOD
PROFESSIONALS

Volume Four:

Tod Browning
Don Siegel

by
Stuart Rosenthal
Judith M. Kass

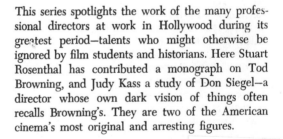

This series spotlights the work of the many professional directors at work in Hollywood during its
greatest period—talents who might otherwise be
ignored by film students and historians. Here Stuart
Rosenthal has contributed a monograph on Tod
Browning, and Judy Kass a study of Don Siegel—a
director whose own dark vision of things often
recalls Browning's. They are two of the American
cinema's most original and arresting figures.

$4.95

In the same series,
produced by THE TANTIVY PRESS
and edited by Peter Cowie:

The Hollywood Professionals

TOD BROWNING

by Stuart Rosenthal

DON SIEGEL

by Judith M. Kass

THE TANTIVY PRESS, LONDON
A. S. BARNES & CO., NEW YORK

FIRST PUBLISHED 1975
Copyright © 1975 by The Tantivy Press
Library of Congress Catalogue Card No. 74-14266
ISBN 0-498-01665-X

SBN 0-904208-95-8 (U.K.)
Printed in the United States of America

Contents

WEST OF ZANZIBAR: *a studio publicity still shows Browning with Chaney in "human duck" costume. This is the prototype of Cleopatra's mutilation in* FREAKS

Tod Browning

Andrew Sarris classifies Tod Browning as "a subject for further research," while a 16mm film catalogue calls him "an unknown director." Although the director's influence has been somewhat peripheral to the mainstream development of the American cinema, it is surprising that he has not drawn more attention than he has, especially from the *auteur* critics. He is certainly one of the most consistent film-makers ever to work in Hollywood.

An interview in the March, 1928, issue of "Motion Picture Classic," published long before the recent vogue in *auteur* criticism, bears testimony to the distinctiveness of his filmic signature.

"In the long run," Joan Dickey began the piece, "it is more than likely that the directors will be recognised as the real authors of the screen. They, rather than the script writers, are the stylists.

"There is Griffith with his confusing mingling of the stuff of Theodore Dreiser and Laura Jean Libbey. There is George Fitzmaurice, who does for pictures something like what Michael Arlen does for literature. There is James Cruze, who is a virilist like Conrad.

"Then there is Tod Browning. Here is a stylist among stylists. Almost a specialist."

At least one meticulous biography of Browning is currently in preparation and should shed new light upon his unusual career. A detailed biographical treatment is clearly beyond the scope of the present study for which a brief sketch of the director's early life will suffice.

Browning was born on 12 July, 1882, in Louisville, Kentucky, and—according to most sources—ran away from home at the age of sixteen without finishing high school. He first joined a circus and later entered vaudeville, touring extensively in such acts as "The

World of Mirth," "Mutt and Jeff" and "Lizzard and Coon." He entered motion pictures in either 1913 or 1914 (depending upon the source) as a comedy actor for Biograph in such films as *Scenting a Terrible Crime*. His films shortly thereafter at Majestic-Reliance included *An Exciting Courtship* and *The Wild Girl*. He took a small part in the modern story of Griffith's *Intolerance*, a film on which he served as an assistant director. It was during this period that he began to write scripts while continuing as an assistant.

His solo directoral debut was on *Jim Bludso* for Fine Arts in 1917. By 1919 he was directing programme films for Universal where he first established contact with Lon Chaney and made an extremely successful series of Universal "Jewels" with Priscilla Dean. Such Dean vehicles as *The White Tiger* and *Outside the Law* are characteristic of the seemingly authentic atmosphere with which Browning instilled his crime melodramas. His convincing portraits of seedy underworld types and other associated low-life hint at a familiarity with that *milieu* and added immeasurably to later efforts like *The Black Bird, The Show* and *The Unholy Three*.

One interesting, but unelaborated, paragraph in the "Motion Picture Classic" interview states that "The story of Tod Browning's two sick, inactive years from the screen is too well known to need detailed repetition. He is quite frank in admitting that he could not get a job because he was otherwise occupied in trying to drink up 'all the bad liquor in the world[1]'". Though the reference hints at morbid colour that might help explain some of Browning's preoccupations on the screen, it is difficult to imagine when these "two sick, inactive years" might have occurred. From 1917 until his last picture, *Miracles for Sale* in 1939, Browning made a total of forty-six features, on a schedule that included at least two movies each year throughout the silent era.

The adjective most frequently applied to Browning's cinema is "obsessional." Although the work of any *auteur* will repeatedly emphasise specific thoughts and ideas, Browning is so aggressive and unrelenting in his pursuit of certain themes that he appears to be neurotically fixated upon them. He is inevitably attracted to situations of moral and sexual frustration. In this, as well as in his preoccupation with interchangeable guilt, interchangeable personalities and patterns of human repulsion and attraction, he coincides remarkably with Chabrol. What sets Browning apart is his abnormal fascination with the deformed creatures who populate his films—a fascination that is not always entirely intellectual, and one in which he takes extreme delight.

Browning expresses his obsessive content in a manner that may be properly described as compulsive. Certain shots, compositions and montages appear again and again in the Browning *oeuvre* and, however appropriate they are to his ideas, they leave an impression of frank repetition. In fact, he has a limited catalogue of both themes and effects from which he compiles each of his pictures. The overall scope of the entire Browning filmography is not significantly broader than that of any single entry in it.

This limitation does serve as an advantage in the critical evaluation of Browning's cinema. Most of his films have not been available until recently; even now, fewer than half of them are easily obtainable, with some very important productions like *London After Midnight* still on the lost lists. The prints that are commercially available are often incomplete. For example, missing footage makes the conclusion of *Where East Is East* incomprehensible in the 16mm print that is offered for rental in the United States. But, because of the constant reiteration, it is possible to make some observations and perhaps even draw some conclusions from the films and fragments that can be seen.

The typical Browning protagonist is a man who has been reduced to the state of an animal. In almost every instance he displays a physical deformity that reflects the mental mutilation he

WEST OF ZANZIBAR: Chaney shares a common nature with a wild chimpanzee

has suffered at the hands of some element of callous society. In *West of Zanzibar* Chaney loses the use of both legs when Barrymore, who is about to run off with Chaney's wife, pushes him off of a balcony. His overwhelming psychic pain is channelled into a search for revenge that dominates him in the same manner that an instinct governs an animal's actions. The bestiality of his nature is underlined in a shot in which "Dead Legs" (as Chaney is now called) playfully hugs a wild chimpanzee. It is the only instant in the film in which he loses his menacing aura. At the same time, his affection for the beast reaffirms that he is basically humane.

THE UNKNOWN: Chaney, in animal fashion, uses his feet as hands

More direct evidence of the animal affinities of Browning characters can be found in their names: "Tiger," the circus trapper in *Where East Is East,* "Cock Robin," the carnival performer in *The Show,* and the title character in *The Black Bird,* to name a few. As animals they act in response to very simple, innate passions, the strongest of which is a lust for retribution. Their steadfast confidence in their own righteousness and their ascetic dedication to their singular goals contributes to the inexhaustible strength which allows them to triumph over those who have made them outcasts.

Alonzo, in *The Unknown,* is among the most rabid and instinctive of Browning's protagonists. Like an animal, he uses feet as hands and, significantly, he chooses animals—horses—as his means for disarticulating his nemesis, Malabar the Strongman. Alonzo's death beneath the horse's hooves, therefore, occurs in his own element. Similarly, animals become the agents of destruction for Tiger in *Where East is East* and Echo in *The Unholy Three*.

The vampire's capacity to change into a bat or wolf at will is the most literal of Browning's animal transformations. Still it is obvious that these incarnations of evil are not meant to be regarded in the same adulatory light as "Tiger" or "Dead Legs". Therefore it is important to recognise that the Browning menagerie distinguishes two classes of animalised man—the righteous beast of prey and the scavengers and vermin.

This is why the protagonist of *The Black Bird* must ultimately fail in his jealous vendetta against Bertie. The Black Bird is a criminal chieftain who uses an alternate identity to evade the law. By twisting and contorting his body, he becomes The Bishop, a crippled clergyman. As his name implies, he falls into the category of scavengers and parasites. Unlike the heroes of *Where East Is East, West of Zanzibar, The Devil-Doll* and *Freaks,* his motivations are corrupt and, in the end, he does not succeed.

Although, in their instinctive behaviour, Browning's heroes are oblivious to the moral contradictions of revenge, they do maintain a latent sense of fairness which influences their dealings with those who have not afflicted them. This is one aspect of Barrymore's willingness to sacrifice his own happiness in *The Devil-Doll* in order to avoid embarrassing his daughter who is ashamed of him. It also accounts for his unwillingness to continue to exploit his "devil dolls" after he has vindicated himself. Chaney trades his own life for that of his daughter in *Where East Is East* and *West of Zanzibar* and risks imprisonment to free the clerk framed by the burglary ring in *The Unholy Three*. The appetite for revenge can be viewed as an extreme of this concern with fairness.

Freaks is the film that is most explicit about the closeness of equitability and retribution. The freaks live by a simple and unequivocable code that one imagines might be the crux of Browning's ideal for society: "Offend one of them and you offend them all." (Browning's other films, however, belie the possibility of practically implementing such an ideal system.) The freaks, as a group, have taken responsibility for the welfare of each individual member. There is no duplicity within their tightly knit community. They want to co-exist harmoniously with the world of the "big people," but if anyone attempts to harm or take advantage of one

FREAKS: the communal solidarity of the freaks demonstrated in a social context, the birth of the bearded lady's baby

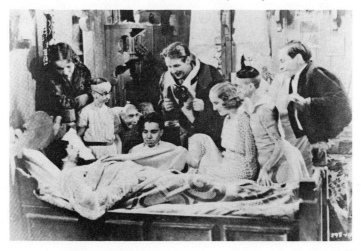

of their number the entire colony responds quickly and surely to
mete out appropriate punishment.

The solidarity of the freaks is a feature introduced to the story
by Browning. It does not occur in "Spurs," the Tod Robbins short
story from which *Freaks* is adapted. Browning's handiwork is also
evident in the fairness that tempers the implementation of their
doctrine. The group does not respond to Cleopatra's disparagement
of Frieda, delaying action against Cleopatra and Hercules until it
has undeniable proof of their intention to murder Hans. Since this
is one of those rare instances in Browning's pictures in which guilt
can be indisputably fixed, the freaks can be totally justified in
their attack. The dwarf in "Spurs" is a hideously arbitrary and
vicious individual compared to the victimised Hans in the film.

Tenacity of willpower is another important trait found in
Browning's central characters. This provides the self-discipline
which drives them relentlessly toward the achievement of their
goals. It also allows them to manipulate those with weaker personalities through a kind of mental control. Feelings of external
thought control are a common delusionary symptom in psychiatric
disease and their presence in Browning's work heightens its obsessional quality.

Barrymore's instruments of revenge in *The Devil-Doll* are tiny,
deadly, living dolls who have no wills of their own and respond to
his telepathic commands. By extension through these miniatures he
is able to dominate his enemies. Even when Barrymore is not in
physical proximity to the on-screen action, his presence is felt
through the claustrophobic quality of the images which are com-
posed with bar-like parallel lines (shadows of venetian blinds,
bookshelves, etc.).

The ability to assume control of another being is equally vital
to *The Unholy Three*. Echo the Ventriloquist delivers testimony
in court through the mouth of Hector, who is being tried for the

LONDON AFTER MIDNIGHT: Chaney as the hypnotist

murder committed by Echo's partners. As the words pour from the witness stand, Browning repeatedly dissolves Echo onto Hector and vice-versa, establishing the performer's complete responsibility for what is being said.

In *Mark of the Vampire* (and *London After Midnight*, of which *Mark of the Vampire* is a re-make) the mode of control is hypnotism. For the purposes of the film, the skill of imposing a trance upon another's mind is not in itself sufficient to unmask the murderer. Barrymore, the inspector, neatly utilises a great deal of rather outlandish cunning to bring his suspect to the point where hyp-

MARK OF THE VAMPIRE: Barrymore as the hypnotist (conversing with Elizabeth Allen)

nosis is used to elicit a confession by re-enactment. While Barrymore, even as an agent of justice, is not the classic Browning animal (just as the basic intention of *Mark of the Vampire* is somewhat removed from Browning's traditional aims), he manipulates his quarry with ease. This is an exaggerated picture of the relative positions of Browning's unswervingly confident protagonists to the men they stalk.

The most awesome powers of control belong to the vampires and Browning's attitude toward these undead poses a particularly intriguing problem. The vampires depend, for support, upon the infirm and innocent elements of society that Browning scorns. They sustain themselves through the blood of the weak whom they can possess, but are vulnerable to those with the determination to resist them. In *Dracula,* Dr. Van Helsing is the character who fits the pattern of the Browning hero because, as the vampire ruefully discovers, his "will is strong."

In the lower levels of society, to which Browning devoted most of his film-making energies, self-reliance, shrewdness and authority are valuable, highly regarded characteristics. Accordingly, Browning has great respect for men who are in command of their circum-

MARK OF THE VAMPIRE (publicity still): the Vampire as predator Carol Borland, Holmes Herbert, and Bela Lugosi

stances. This esteem is constant and irrespective of the moral nature of their activities. This serves as one explanation for Browning's attraction to such grossly debased characters as Alonzo in *The Unknown,* Black Mike Silva in *Outside the Law* and Cock Robin in *The Show.* Consistent with the moral framework of Browning's films, the Black Bird is necessarily doomed. The director, however, shows no reluctance in indicating substantial admiration for him with respect to specific character traits. Dan Tate (the Black Bird's given name) affects an air of disdainful aloofness that separates him from those in the slum circles in which he moves. The picture opens with a "sea of faces" montage, a sampling of the pathetic types who populate the Limehouse district. This is followed immediately by a cut to Chaney entering a darkened room, far removed from this stream of humanity. Except in moments of anger, he generally displays a detached arrogance, reflecting his attitude of being above the concerns of everyday life in his neighbourhood. The gullible and somewhat faithless lovers easily fall for the Black Bird's scheme to turn them against each other. The audience is never seriously engaged by the romance, nor is it particularly chagrined by Tate's attempt to destroy it. The young couple functions primarily as a plotting device and as a foil to the Black Bird's superior cunning. When Tate sustains his fatal injury and is painfully trapped in the body of the crippled mission-house keeper, he dies repeating to himself, "I'm foolin' em, I'm foolin' em, I'm foolin' em." His claim, useless to him as it is, is verified when the indigents who discover his body remark, "God will be good to you, Bishop, because you were good to us." This last irony constitutes an affirmation of Browning's feeling that in spite of Tate's malfeasance, for which he received proper punishment, his aggressiveness and power over others place him a cut above those with whom he was in contact. A major element of Browning's obsession is an appreciation of adeptness at "fooling the suckers." The grotesque types who view the sideshows in *The Unholy Three* and *The Show* are typical of Browning's view of the "suckers" who are, in both cases, being taken in by the film's star.

In the screen personality of Lon Chaney, Browning found the perfect embodiment of the type of character that interested him. Chaney was experienced in playing "tough guys." He had a reputation for immersing himself in his roles to the fullest possible extent. Stories about the extremes to which he would go in utilising painful make-up and devices have become part of the Hollywood legend. "You probably read how much he [Chaney] suffers in some of his make-ups," Browning says in the "Motion Picture Classic" interview. "That isn't publicity. He will do anything, permit almost anything to be done to him, for the sake of his pictures." Chaney's unconditional dedication to his acting gave his characterisations the extraordinary intensity that was absolutely essential to the credibility of Browning's creations.

The ten films that Browning and Chaney made together were the most successful of either's career. In these films one can sense a personal rapport between the actor and the director which must have been deeper than a mere professional respect. The conjecture that Browning used Chaney as a vent for his own frustrations is not, as we shall see, unreasonable. Chaney demonstrated great sensitivity to the feelings and drives of the outcasts Browning devised for him to play. Browning may well be the only film-maker who saw Chaney as more than an attention-getting gimmick. While many of Chaney's films for other directors involve tales of retribution, only in the Browning vehicles is he endowed with substantial human complexity. Most frequently he is either the unfortunate victim of others—like Quasimodo or the "He" of *He Who Gets Slapped*—or simply a madman—like Erik (*The Phantom of the Opera*) or Blizzard, the gangster with the blood clot on his brain in *The Penalty*.

He Who Gets Slapped when contrasted with *West of Zanzibar* provides an enlightening illustration of how Browning's use of Chaney differs from that of another director in a film with a revenge theme. In *He Who Gets Slapped*, a product of Victor Sjöström's American period, Chaney is a scientist whose wife steals his life's research and gives it to her lover, Chaney's best friend. When Chaney protests that the paper presented to a scientific body by his erstwhile friend is actually his own work, he is heckled into professional obscurity. Shattered, Chaney finds anonymity under the name of "He" and becomes a circus clown with an act that requires him to be repeatedly slapped by other clowns and to respond with a laugh. In the end, He unleashes a lion upon his former colleague. This is entirely a spur of the moment act.

Although He and Dead Legs have suffered devastating betrayals, their responses are exactly opposite. A Browning hero would never feel He's compulsion to symbolically relive a moment of humiliation. Instead of taking the philosophical route of subjugating himself to his frustration, Browning's Chaney opts for the primitive satisfaction of striking back, converting his emotional upheaval into a source of primal strength. The viewer, empathising with the protagonist, is shocked at the realisation of his own potential for maniacally harnessing the power of his sense of outrage. This is one of the reasons why *West of Zanzibar* and Chaney's other Browning films are so much more disturbing than the horror mysteries he made with other directors.

Browning was also unique in his recognition of the expressive potential of Chaney's face which could be as plastically agile as his body. Browning's close-ups of Chaney seldom portray a single emotion. What is important to a Browning characterisation is the capacity for sudden, rapid changes in affect, rather than the emotions themselves. Chaney would often progress from amusement to merriment to gloating to puzzlement to surprise and then through

anger into a state of rage in a single close shot. In *West of Zanzibar,*
upon learning that his wife never really left with Barrymore, he
slides from incredulity to tears when a moment before he was
mirthfully smug as he savoured his revenge. A similar facial meta-
morphis occurs in *The Unknown* when Joan Crawford reveals
her affair with the strongman. It is slower and even more controlled
than the change in *West of Zanzibar,* and, consequently, introduces
an element of tension.

*THE BLACK BIRD: Chaney, aloof and arrogant when confronted by
Dolores Lloyd (courtesy M-G-M and Films Inc., U.S.A.)*

Browning helps to keep the development of *The Black Bird* taut by employing Chaney's face as an index of the rapidly oscillating mood of the title character. Chaney is the key person who will determine the fates of West End Bertie and Fifi. The plasticity of his facial expression belies to the audience the spirit of co-operation he offers the young couple. In addition, the internal explosiveness monitored in his face is a constant reminder of the danger represented by his presence.

In *The Road to Mandalay* a rapid emotional alteration reflected in Chaney's face signals a change in direction for the story. As Singapore Joe jubilantly prepares a practical joke for the oily Charlie Wing, his face undergoes a transition from mischievousness to amazement to anger ending in threatening hostility when he finds his daughter in the room with his brother and the "Admiral." This sets the tone for the film's final movement which culminates with the Oriental's harrowing sexual advance and Joe's death. Everything preceding this moment is a treatment of a frustrated romance—in effect, a family quarrel. Chaney's face is used structurally in this case as a visual pivot to redirect the mood.

Frequently it is possible to simultaneously read two reactions in Chaney's face. An early glimpse of the Black Bird watching Madame Fifi's act establishes first his entrancement with the performer and then his active enthusiasm as he claps his hands with sweeping movements and whistles through his teeth. At the same time he appears to be inwardly chortling, providing a first intimation that he sees her as a challenge—a subject for conquest—and is about to make a move.

In another statement, Van Tate is scoffing at Bertie's offer to buy back a stolen diamond necklace. Then Fifi appears at their table with the wilted violets that Chaney had delivered to her dressing room. Chaney's eyes narrow sinisterly as he watches Bertie purchase fresh flowers. The rising anger in what might be described

as his "clenched" eyelids then blossoms unexpectedly and discon-
certingly into a broad, self-assured, all-knowing smile. He removes
the wilted violet that Fifi had placed in his rival's lapel and re-
places it with one of the fresh plants. As soon as Bertie has departed,
he turns sullen and the camera dwells upon him for several seconds.
Abruptly flying into a rage, he smashes the glass in front of him.
The facial manoeuvring serves as an anticipatory period preceding
an uncontainable seizure, conditioning in the viewer a reaction of
discomfort to a Chaney smile.

"When I am working on a story for Chaney," Browning said
in the "Motion Picture Classic" interview, "I never think of the
plot. That follows of itself after you have conceived a characterisation."

Having a characterisation in mind, Browning built his films by
generating an elaborately interlocking structure of frustration
around that individual. Frustration is Browning's dominant theme.
It occurs in several distinct patterns, each of which can be recognised
in almost every Browning film. These modes of frustration include:

1. *Reality versus Appearance.* The standard criteria by which we
form "first impressions" are useless in Browning's universe. Physical
beauty and positions of public trust are frequently *façades* for the
most reprehensible villains.

2. *Sexual Frustration.* In Browning's films a man's offspring represent extensions of his own sexuality. The father-child relationship
is especially sacred. An insult to a son or daughter is also an insult
to the parent, and *vice versa.* Under these conditions bastardy is
a particularly intolerable state. Sexual frustration in Browning's
work may be either experienced first hand or indirectly, through
a close relative.

3. *Conflict of Two Opposing Tendencies within an Individual.*
This is an internal, identity-related frustration. It may be mani-

23

fested by the use of alter egos or by the symbolic separation of the pair of qualities into two individuals.

4. *Inability to Assign Guilt.* Any system of justice, especially the Browning hero's revenge drive, is frustrated by situations in which guilt cannot be clearly fixed. In such instances the avenger himself must often sin in order to punish the sins of others.

It is worthwhile to discuss each of these forms of frustration separately before seeing how they work together in *Fast Workers*.

1. *REALITY VERSUS APPEARANCE*

The bulk of *Freaks* is spent dispelling the viewer's initial revulsion to the title characters. They are shown in the activities of normal life—eating, chatting, playing, working, arranging matrimony and celebrating the birth of a child. The freaks surmount their handicaps by going through sets of bizarre movements. Browning presents these in a matter-of-fact manner rather than as tricks. The involved procedure used by the Human Torso, a man without arms or legs, to light his cigarette is handled as incidental action in a contrived dialogue scene. At the other end of the scale, Browning prevents his audience from pitying the freaks by using their deformities as the basis for a great deal of black humour.

Running countercurrent to the normalisation of the freaks is the bestialising of Cleopatra, the trapeze artist, and of her boyfriend, Hercules the Strongman. In contradistinction to their strange circus colleagues, these two are opportunistic, insensitive, unscrupulous and without allegiance to anyone except themselves. Physical beauty masking perversity is identical to the usual Browning premise of respectability covering corruption.

This is the formula used in *Where East Is East*. Tiger's thorny face masks a wealth of kindness, sensitivity and abiding paternal love. But behind the exotic beauty of Madame de Silva lies an unctuous, sinister manner and callous spitefulness. The horrific "One Eyed Joe" in *The Road to Mandalay* has much in common with Tiger in that his intention is always to provide for and protect his daughter, even to the point of concealing his identity from her and breaking up her wedding. Obviously, the adorable baby in *The Unholy Three* is far from sweet and innocent, while kindly Mrs. O'Grady is actually a criminal mastermind. To further the irony, the formidable-looking Echo is ultimately shown to have a soft spot for Rosie and Hector.

The pattern is seen again in *The Devil-Doll* when Lionel Barrymore breaks out of prison in order to destroy the three bankers who framed him for the embezzlement they committed. Barrymore's concern for his daughter and refusal to misuse his powers mark him as a good man. Yet he is hunted as a dangerous felon while the three villains live as leading citizens of the community. Interestingly, Browning drags out Chaney's old lady make-up from *The Unholy Three* as a disguise for Barrymore while he goes about his work of angry destruction. But when his revenge is complete, like Echo, he demonstrates a highly beneficent nature. Echo made up as the grandmother bears a remarkable resemblance to Barrymore disguised as the elderly woman who sells dolls in *The Devil-Doll*. This is further evidence of the interchangeability of Browning's heroes, all of whom would act identically if given the same set of circumstances.

2. SEXUAL FRUSTRATION

Browning regularly introduces the theme of secondary or "indirect" sexual frustration through the plot device of a parent who is unaware of the identity of his own child, or the reverse situation. Singapore Joe in *Road to Mandalay* is so ugly that he feels his daughter (who, indeed, abhors that hideous man when he patron-

THE UNHOLY THREE: Chaney in "grandmother" make-up

ises the store in which she clerks) would be ashamed if she were aware of their kinship. The struggle that results when the Admiral, one of Joe's smuggling colleagues, announces his plan to wed her has overtones of a fight to maintain the sexual integrity of the family. When this conflict is juxtaposed with Joe's efforts to hold his position as top dog in the local underworld, the infighting among the hoodlums acquires the aspect of a battle for sexual supremacy. Keeping the community of gangsters under control becomes primarily a matter of *machismo*.

Lionel Barrymore, in *The Devil-Doll,* makes a similar attempt to protect his daughter from embarrassment and unhappiness by concealing his identity from her even after he has been cleared of the embezzlement. In an ironic way, by denying himself his daughter, he is punishing himself for the crimes (murder and responsibility for a man's paralysis) that he committed in the course of his self-exoneration. Clearly, the most deplorable consequence of his being framed was not the loss of his reputation or the years he spent in prison, but the alienation of his daughter's love and respect.

Variations of the "unknown parentage" *motif* are found in *The Show* and *White Tiger.* In the former film, the old blind man who lives with Salome mistakes John Gilbert for his lost son. Salome, who is in love with Gilbert despite his inattention, encourages him to continue the charade. Though the masquerade is designed to give the old man peace of mind, the excitement proves too much for him. He falls dead just at the moment his real son is being executed as a criminal in the prison courtyard across the street. Only then does Gilbert learn that the elderly man was Salome's father. The normally contemptuous Gilbert then lavishes praise upon the girl for her steadfast loyalty and self-sacrificing attitude toward her father.

Like the native death code in *West of Zanzibar* which requires a man's demise to be followed by the death of his wife or child, the blind man's end is indicative of Browning's insistence upon the integrity of the family line. Frequently, a father will sacrifice himself for the maintainence of his lineage. The *pièce de resistance* of Dead Legs's plot is to taunt Barrymore in his final hours with the impending murder of the girl he believes is his enemy's daughter. When he learns that the girl is in reality, his own offspring, he unsuccessfully risks his own life, assuring her safety. To prevent her from being tainted by her father's depravity Barrymore decides that she must never learn the truth about their relationship. This is also the rationale for one part of Paul Lavond's final denial of his daughter in *The Devil-Doll*. Tiger, in *Where East Is East*, has his entire life tied up in his daughter, Toyo, and is very ill at ease over her proposed marriage to Bobby Bailey until Bailey demonstrates his manliness by fending off an escaped tiger. Singapore Joe, who hopes to upgrade himself by having a surgeon repair his face, tries to prevent his daughter's marriage to one of his gangster cohorts by kidnapping the bridegroom.

The same film displays a racist abhorrence of sexual pollution through miscegenation in English Charlie Wing's attempt to rape the white woman. This is an echo of the Black Bird's forthright stand in sending the young girl home from the show bar. "You want me to tell your dad you're out with a Chink?" he asks. Overtones of this sort pervade *West of Zanzibar* as the mindless natives with their muscular, black, glistening bodies lurk about Chaney's establishment waiting for his order to carry the white daughter to her death.

The disruption of family ties in *White Tiger* is more oblique and, in a sense, more latently perverse. The double-crossing of Mike Donovan by his lieutenant, Hawkes, results not only in Donovan's being gunned down, but in the separation of his two youngsters, Roy and Sylvia. Before the score can be settled many years

WHERE EAST IS EAST: Chaney plays "tiger" with his daughter (Lupe Velez)

WEST OF ZANZIBAR: implicit racist threat of miscegenation as the natives come to sacrifice Chaney's daughter (courtesy Kevin Brownlow)

later, the brother and sister must be reunited, even though they are unaware of each other's identity. Although, from their initial encounter at the wax museum, their relationship maintains a brotherly/sisterly tone, one is always at least vaguely aware of its potentially incestuous implications. Their admiration for each other as professionals in larceny closely resembles Echo and Rosie's camaraderie in *The Unholy Three*, and Roy's suspicions about Longworth, the odd gentleman in whom Sylvia shows considerable interest, is handled in a way not unlike Echo's jealous distrust of Hector.

The reversion to an animalistic state in Browning's cinema functions as a way of acquiring raw power to be used as a means of sexual assertion. The incident that prompts the regression and search for vengeance is, in almost every case, sexual in nature. Dead Legs's wife is stolen and (he believes) impregnated by an adulterous lover. Gunner (in *Fast Workers*) feels humiliated after his new bride is exposed as something other than the young innocent he assumed her to be. The strongman distracts the affections of Joan Crawford from Alonzo in *The Unknown* and Bertie takes the upper hand over the Black Bird in their rivalry for Fifi. Tiger's bitterness in *Where East Is East* is the result of disgust at Madame de Silva's past and present treachery. All of these men are striving

THE UNKNOWN: the circus setting

THE UNKNOWN: Alonzo and his bifid thumb

desperately to overcome their inner embarrassment and, by reveng-
ing themselves, re-establish their personal feelings of sexual dominance.

The Unknown defines a sexual basis for the frustration theme
of the entire Browning-Chaney cycle and relates it directly to the
star's inevitable physical deformity. Chaney plays Alonzo, "the
Armless Wonder," a circus performer who uses his feet to throw
knives at Joan Crawford, the circus owner's daughter. Only his assistant, a hunchback dwarf, knows that Alonzo is a fake. He not
only has arms, but one of his hands has a double thumb. He is
infatuated with Crawford who has a neurotic aversion to being

handled by men and, naturally, an armless man is the only lover she can abide. One night, in the course of an argument, Alonzo strangles the circus owner. Joan Crawford, witnessing the murder from a window, sees only that the assailant has an extra thumb. The knife-thrower is safe from suspicion as long as no one knows he has arms, but if he proceeds to marry, his wife will discover his secret. He deals with the dilemma by having his arms amputated, but while he is in the hospital Joan Crawford overcomes her phobia and falls in love with Malabar, the strongman. The venomous Alonzo plots to have a team of horses tear the strongman's arms from his body, but he slips and is trampled to death while trying to execute his plan. The amputations take on the significance of castration and Joan Crawford's fear of being grabbed by men is a bizarre (and self-defeating) psychosexual dysfunction in which she is aroused only by "sexless" men. Alonzo is a figure of heightened sexual prowess, understood not only from the supernumerary thumb but from the fact that, even with his arms tethered tightly to his body, he is able to function at an above-normal level. At one point, he uses his foot to light and smoke a cigarette although his arms are hanging freely at his side. "You forget that you have arms," Cojo, his dwarf valet, reminds him.

As Browning approached the peak of his career, the sexual undercurrents of his films became less and less covert. While *Freaks* affords the most explicit expression of the fears that haunt the background of all his pictures, *Dracula* borders upon the surreal as an evocation of repressed sexual horror. From Kipling's poem and Theda Bara to the Hammer film formula and Polanski's satire of vampire conventions, the term "vampire" has denoted an unholy association between death and sex. With regard to the ghoul itself, the nocturnal blood lust equates to necrophilic passion and the demon appears as a pestilent incubus, preying at night upon sleeping female innocence and turning his victims, through the

touch of his fangs, into willing slaves. Dracula was originally billed as "The strangest love story of all."

Though updated from Bram Stoker's novel, the Browning version of Dracula retains the Victorian formality of the original source in the relationships among the normal characters. In this atmosphere the seething, unstoppable evil personified by the Count is a materialisation of Victorian morality's greatest dread. David Manners's stiffness and ineffectuality in his dealings with his *fiancée* are sheer impotence in contrast to Dracula's irresistible power. By these standards it is certain that, as Lugosi tells Lucy as the lights dim at the opera, "There are far worse things awaiting man than death!" It is possible to infer another parallel to the inner conflict of sexual repression when Van Helsing notes that "The strength of the vampire is that people will not believe in him."

Sexual frustration is the very essence of *Freaks*. The central event—the marriage of Hans, the dwarf, to Cleopatra, the statuesque trapeze artiste—is a collision of absolute sexual opposites—the attempted consummation of an impossible union. An early scene in which Hans encounters the aerialist makes the contradiction of their pairing clear. Cleopatra towers over the miniscule Hans. She speaks in coarse, booming tones while the dwarf has a high wavering voice. Cleopatra is seductive, mature, cunning and self-assured in contrast to Hans who looks like a baby and is uncertain of her response to his guilelessly open admiration. In viewing them we are struck primarily by the gross incongruity of the pair, but our reaction to the scene is a product of the two mutually exclusive points of view that are comprised in it. For Hans, a chance at the big lady is a wild goal beyond reach or reason, representing the fulfilment of his most extravagant fantasies. The smug trapeze performer contemptuously regards the midget as an opportunity to

Facing page: Olga Baclanova and Harry Earles—collision of absolute sexual opposites—in FREAKS

enjoy the kind of cruel sexual jest upon which she thrives.

It is here that Browning justifies the disruption of an individual's sexual equanimity as a cause for retaliation. Cleopatra's decision to wed the dwarf for his wealth and then dispose of him is not, in itself, a significant advance in villainy. In the context of the film, her most heinous crime is committed when she teases Hans by provocatively dropping her cape to the floor and then gleefully kneels to allow her victim to replace it upon her shoulders. The decision to commit a murder is merely the natural development of her eagerness to taunt and sexually belittle the dwarf. This kind of exploitation appears more obscene by far than the fairly clean act of homicide.

Another view of Cleopatra as sexual marauder is afforded by her treatment of Frieda, Hans's *fiancée*. Their first encounter takes place when Cleopatra maliciously irritates the female dwarf by playing with her skirts; the second occurs when Frieda stops by the aerialist's wagon to beg her to stop making a laughingstock of Hans. In each case Cleopatra is reassuring herself of her sexual superiority. Like Hercules, who is constantly displaying his strength and seeking new ways to underline his virility, Cleopatra's confidence depends upon continual reconfirmation of her ability to defeat any sexual adversary—real or potential.

Contrast the insecurity of the normal-sized leads with the unruffled attitudes of the Freaks. They have accepted their limitations and adapted to them. Even the individuals with radical amputations (which, as elsewhere in Browning, carry strong connotations of castration) have adjusted marvellously to their physical constraints, using arms as legs and mouths as hands. Beyond this, many of the freaks represent reconciliations of prevalent sexual apprehensions. Beside the "half-man, half-woman" there is the comically complaisant attitude toward a kind of miscegenation in the birth of a child to the "human skeleton" and the bearded fat

LONDON AFTER MIDNIGHT: Chaney as the vampire, the hypnotist's alter ego (courtesy Kevin Brownlow)

lady. Phroso tells the beautiful Venus, without a trace of wistfulness, "You should have caught me before my operation." Even Roscoe Ates is serious when he says to the *fiancée* of his Siamese twin bride-to-be's sister, "You must come to visit us sometime too."

The wedding feast is the definitive confrontation between the big villains and the freaks. The continual, spontaneous motion of

37

the freaks visually indicates the magnitude of their energy and power. It offsets the drunken, derisive laughter of Cleopatra and Hercules as they howl over the implementation of their scheme to poison the new husband. Cleopatra's first experience with the fully mustered strength of the sideshow performers marks a change in the direction of the film's sexual threat. Initially, Cleopatra is delighted with her little joke ("Nothing like being different," she told Frieda earlier. "Imagine that—Cleopatra, Queen of the Air, married to a dwarf!!") But when the weird, rhythmic, almost pagan initiation ritual begins, her confidence is shattered and her fear expresses itself as revulsion. She regains her footing by renewed humiliation of Hans after Hercules has ordered the gathering to break up.

If, as some psychiatrists contend, our natural aversion to the deformed is based upon a deep-seated fear that the same could happen to us, then the wedding feast represents the hard materialisation of a threat that has been implicit throughout the film. In the Browning frame of reference, this is a sexual threat which is fully realised by the freaks' reprisal. Cleopatra is transformed into an astounding freak—a sexless chicken. The original ending in which the strongman was emasculated is further in keeping with the dark sexual themes of the picture.

3. CONFLICT OF OPPOSING TENDENCIES WITHIN AN INDIVIDUAL

Lon Chaney is often lauded as an actor capable of developing a completely different personality for each new role. In his Browning films, however, all the characters he portrays are plugged into a single consciousness created and imposed upon them by the director. When Chaney plays two totally dissimilar parts in a single picture, each of his characters embodies one of two opposing tendencies found in the overall concept of the Browning protagonist. The Jekyll and Hyde fashion in which one Chaney character thwarts the other again underlines the intractable frustration that Browning projected onto his star. In the end, the Black Bird breaks his back and is trapped in the body of the Bishop. In the finale of *Outside the Law*, Chaney impersonates both the gentle Oriental and the hard-boiled mobster he shoots. Echo, the criminal ventriloquist of *The Unholy Three*, dons the clothes of a kindly old woman to case potential robbery sites. The detective in *London After Midnight* ensnares a murder suspect with an impersonation of a grinning vampire.

The Black Bird's masquerade as the Bishop succeeds primarily because the Bishop's face so believably reflects a profound spiritual suffering that is absolutely foreign to the title character. When Bertie and Fifi come to the sham clergyman for aid, Tate slips momentarily out of character, regarding them suspiciously out of the corners of his eyes and bringing his mouth into a tight little curl. The face assures us that this is the underworld kingpin and not the sympathetic person that the twisted limbs and clerical garb would seem to indicate. Physical disfiguration for Browning is a sign of teeming internal chaos and by no means denotes a pure or sympathetic creature. In Browning's films real suffering brings out the dangerous qualities in a man. Whatever good deed he may eventually do is the result of his initial strength of character and in spite of the externally imposed suffering which forces men like Dead Legs and Paul Lavond (in *The Devil-Doll*) into new and deeper guilt. Lavond is a snarling, hateful man. Dead Legs is one of the ugliest and most incorrigible of Browning's heroes. The Bishop's forlorn expression reveals a propensity for passive suffering, placing him closer to Sjöström's He the Clown than to Lavond or Dead Legs. Since this inclination toward self sub-

jugation is incompatible with the assertive traits that Browning prizes, Dan Tate is split into two. The phoney suffering and soft manner go into one package, the Bishop, while scornful aggressiveness and rough-hewn features are combined in the Black Bird.

Browning sometimes uses another person or group of people to represent a trait that is antagonistic to the basic impulses of the central character. This approach both accentuates the lead's lack of reliance upon the segregated characteristic and increases the probability of a clash between the two tendencies. The image of Alonzo as a super-virile, purely physical creature motivated entirely by elementary animal passions is furthered by the presence of John George, who plays Cojo, the hunchback assistant. Cojo is frequently pictured trailing behind his master, attired in an identical hat and cape. In these shots he looks like a miniature version of Alonzo himself. It is Cojo who points out to the eager Alonzo that his contemplated marriage would result in the discovery of his arms and his incrimination. The dwarf, dressed like Alonzo but lacking his physical endowments, serves as an appendage of intelligence, separated completely from the knife thrower's body. In *Freaks* the eyes of the freaks have the effect of an external conscience as they peer out of the dark from beneath the wagons at the voluptuous, unfeeling Cleopatra, reminding her of her guilt. Gunner (in *Fast Workers*) feels compelled to expose all the women for whom the easily infatuated Bucker Reilly falls. In each of these cases the dominant disposition of a character is frustrated by a repressed (indicated by physical dissociation) countertendency.

Opposite: the Bishop's face in THE BLACK BIRD reflects profound spiritual suffering. Chaney as "The Black Bird's" alter ego.

THE UNKNOWN: Chaney and John George. The dwarf represents a separate mentality for Alonzo

4. INABILITY TO ASSIGN GUILT

In the Browning canon *Freaks* is almost allegorical in that it singles out individuals about whose guilt there can be no doubt. Justice is perfectly served because retribution is meted out only for the absolute crime of "attempted murder," but the sentence is such that it appropriately covers the crime of sexual humiliation. Usually, however, there is situational confusion in assigning guilt in Browning's stories. This generates a level of frustration that is directly concerned with the instinctive plane of justice the Browning films seek.

Alonzo, in *The Unknown,* commits what amounts to an act of self-castration. He is driven to that point by Estrellita (Joan Crawford), who not only leads him into a position in which it is desirable to be without arms but, having brought him there, arbitrarily reverses herself after the damage is irreparable. "Estrellita," a title reads, "wishes God has taken the arms from all men." She is, accordingly, both the film's provoker and the mortal enemy of the kind of physical man Chaney represents—even though she is unaware that Alonzo is exactly the sort she most despises.

In regarding Estrellita's betrayal, it is easy to overlook the fact that Alonzo's guilt is immaterial to his yearning for her. He has murdered a man and thus created a whole new set of circumstances under which armlessness is an asset. He has two reasons, then, for blackmailing the doctor into surgically removing his upper extremities. The first is entirely of his own making while the other results from his victimisation at the hands of his maladjusted female ideal. The implication that Alonzo's affair with Estrellita was a contributing factor in maintaining the tension between him and the circus owner further obfuscates the question of whether the major responsibility for his ultimate solution rests primarily with Alonzo or with Estrellita.

Another facet in this intricate structure of guilt arises from Alonzo's choice of Malabar as the target for retribution. Logically, Alonzo's anger should be directed toward the girl, not the strongman. But in a film in which the sexual tension is almost palpable, it does not seem unreasonable to accept the unification of Estrellita and Malabar as a medium by which the blame may be transferred, or at least redistributed. On symbolic grounds it is fitting that Alonzo should avenge his own castration by attacking a figure of exaggerated masculinity, while the "arm for an arm" punishment, as an illusion of justice, mirrors Alonzo's illusion of the strongman's guilt. In the long view, it is these ambiguous and outrageously twisted threads of guilt and justice that makes *The Unknown* so audacious.

West of Zanzibar reaches the peak of its psychological horror when Chaney discovers that the girl he is using as a pawn in his revenge scheme is his own daughter. Dead Legs undertook his mission of revenge with complete confidence in the righteousness of his cause. Now he is suddenly overwhelmed by the realisation of his own guilt. That Barrymore committed the initial transgression in no way diminishes that guilt. As in *The Unknown* and *The Devil-Doll,* a zealous attempt to secure justice turns itself into a new crime. In *The Road to Mandalay* the intertitle statement attributed to Joe summarises the plight of Alonzo, Paul Lavond and Dead Legs. It refers to "the evil men like us eternally carry in our souls. We've sunk too low and no longer will God let us rise back."

In *Fast Workers* the four varieties of frustration are so well integrated among themselves that it is difficult, if not impossible, to say where one ends and another begins. These interrelations make it one of the most perplexing of Browning's films, especially with regard to morality and justice. The title itself is *double entendre,* referring both to the construction workers skill at riveting and to their style with women. Each of the three principals is, to one extent or another, at fault in the series of events that lead to Bucker's premeditatedly allowing Gunner to fall off a skyscraper.

Bucker, by virtue of his gullibility, is the weakest of the trio. He is perpetually being conned into marriage by the "gold-digging" women he uses and is dependent upon his pal Gunner to expose them. Their standard technique for demonstrating infidelity is for Gunner to seduce the girl and report to Bucker. It is apparent, as Bucker tells his laughing co-workers how they kicked the last girl "down the hall, through the lobby and out the door," that they approach their women with a ruthless double standard.

Mary is one of Gunner's old girls who so captivates Bucker that he hastily marries her without consulting his usual ally. While she does use some imaginative chicanery to entrap her prospective husband and certainly displays a good deal of interest in his money (upon learning that he has saved $500, she exclaims "Oh, you darling!!"), she exhibits a genuine fondness for Bucker. The fact that she is a victim of the depression tends further to distort the moral issues. Her desire to improve her condition in difficult times is easily appreciated. The status of her hopes for the future are clarified after she bails Gunner, the man she really loves, out of jail with money borrowed from the unknowing Bucker. "You're a nice kid," Gunner tells her, "the sweetest in the world, but don't pull that forever and ever stuff on me. Makes me wanna reach for my hat."

Gunner's motivation for disclosing Mary's background to Bucker is highly suspect. Ostensibly it is an act of friendship to a man who needs to be protected from his own lack of scepticism. Mary, however, means no harm to her husband, who is quite satisfied and elated over the marriage. Gunner acts in self-interest when he persuades Mary to spend the weekend with him in New Orleans while Bucker believes she is attending her grandmother's funeral. His presentation of photographs of the weekend to Bucker is a gesture of sexual humiliation as vicious in spirit as Bucker's reaction, an attempt at murder.

After the weekend, Mary and Gunner find themselves in an extraordinarily frustrating dilemma. Gunner fels slighted by Mary for whom he obviously has some feeling. If he "shows her up" he will have obtained satisfaction for what he sees as her betrayal of him, and will, to his mind, have rescued the folly-prone Bucker. But, if he does not interfere, he will feel that he has let down his best friend, and he will continue to seethe over Mary. He reacts to this frustration with sudden violence, just as Chaney might have done, by putting his fist through a pane of window glass. Mary interprets Gunner's sullen irritability, with some insight, as unhappiness that he has permanently lost her. She too, is experiencing a tinge of regret. She is already secretly married to Bucker, but feels she has lost what may have been a chance to get Gunner.

Fast Workers is Browning's final cynical word on the impossibility of an individual obtaining justice, however righteous his cause, without critically sullying himself. Superficially things have been set right. Gunner and Bucker are again friends and, together are equal to any wily female. Yet Gunner, the individual who is most culpable, finds himself in the most secure position (with only a few broken bones), while the basically well intentioned Mary is rejected and condemned by both men.

For the most part, Browning's films grip their audience by conditioning it to expect some harrowing event and then holding it at the point of anticipation. The stories are fashioned around the central character and most of our dread springs from fear for or of him. Browning punctuates these formations of psychological suspense with moments of outright shock. His set procedure for generating horror is quickly to throw the audience off balance, overwhelm it with some terrible threat and then cut away abruptly to let the viewer draw his own conclusions. The audience (which has already been put on edge by the film's intrinsic tension) is disconcerted by an unexpected change in camera angle or perspective. These alterations come as a jolt in contrast to the simple three-shot narrative style used for the rest of the film. One reacts not only to the action when Barrymore and John Gilbert are trapped inside a closet with a poisonous iguana in *The Show*, but also to the unexpected shift from a succession of head-on shots to a high angle one. The same can be said of the change of framing when

WEST OF ZANZIBAR: *Chaney as "Dead Legs." Camera placement accentuates slithering movements (courtesy M-G-M and Films Inc., U.S.A.)*

Harry Earles uncages the gorilla in *The Unholy Three*. First we see the ape through a keyhole, and then it appears framed in the open door in a long shot of the room. The climax of *The Unknown* is exceptional for Browning in that it cuts between several camera set-ups.

Browning gets extra fright mileage from his characters' animal transformations by suddenly changing the visual frame of reference to one that puts the viewer on the same level as the beast on the screen, thereby making him vulnerable to it. This is most commonly accomplished by tilting up the camera at floor level just in front of its moving subject. This shot markedly accentuates crawling and slithering movements and is seen at its most memorable in *Dracula* as a delighted Dwight Frye crawls toward the serving lady who has just fainted. It is also effective in the first single shot of the "half-man" in *Freaks* and when applied to Chaney on the ground in *West of Zanzibar*. An analogue of the shot using real animals occurs in *The Devil-Doll* and *The Show* when a St. Bernard and a herd of sheep, respectively, stroll directly into the camera. Then, too, there is the terrifically frightening close-up of Dracula's bright white face with its gleaming parted lips, moving down almost on top of the lens as it dives for its victim's throat.

Occasionally, shock set-pieces are strategically planted to stun the filmgoer and make him more inclined to accept whatever incredible turn of events may follow. "The thing you have to be most careful of in a mystery story," Browning is quoted in the "Motion Picture Classic" interview, "is not to let it verge on the comic. If a thing gets too gruesome and too horrible, it gets beyond the limits of the average imagination and the audience laughs. It may sound incongruous, but mystery must be made plausible." This explains the necessity for making the decapitation of John Gilbert in *The Show*—one of the most disquieting bits of business in any Browning feature—a flight of Lionel Barrymore's imagination. Through this device Browning can indulge his taste for the absurd-macabre and still numb his audience without sending it into disbelief.

THE SHOW: Browning sets up a moment of shock as he instructs Rene Adore to gaze at John Gilbert's head in the decapitation sequence

Miracles for Sale, the only Browning production that really looks like an M-G-M studio job, begins with an inspired jolt which catches the viewer completely offguard. On the sideline of a battle-field an Oriental military officer chides a beautiful female spy for having dispatched intelligence that led to the bombing of a school-house. He orders her placed in a child's coffin ("You understand why we only have small coffins available," he sneers) with her head and feet protruding from either end, and tells his men to machine-gun the casket in half. After the grisly order has been carried out, to the viewer's amazement, it is revealed that the execution is merely a new variation on the traditional "sawing a woman in half" stunt. The illusion is being offered for sale by

49

Robert Young, a purveyor of magician's paraphernalia. The remainder of Browning's swan song, regrettably, is a fairly routine mystery against a background of the occult.

The climax of *Freaks* probably achieves the most sustained level of high-pitched terror of any Browning picture. The tension begins to accrue when the ubiquitous aberrations start to appear behind every door, window and wagon wheel, like a force of inevitable doom. The horror builds from there in short, staccato shocks as their macabre bodies pull themselves through the mud between flashes of lightning. Toward the end of the sequence their familiar forms are barely recognisable as they scramble in jerky, energetic movements to carve up their victims.

The technique that Browning used for constructing instants of horror in his silent films was workably carried over into the sound era. It is apparent that Browning conceived horror primarily in visual terms. The track behind the bloodsucking activities in *Dracula* carries only distant street or wildlife sounds and the devil dolls do their work in almost absolute silence. These two films, as well as *Mark of the Vampire,* rely upon a minimum of mood music. The track-in on Cleopatra as she seizes upon her plan to murder Hans is, in itself, much more unsettling than her "dwarfs are not strong" speech. The silent, identical camera movement in *Fast Workers,* when Mary realises that Bucker is contemplating murder, is positively chilling. Even in a fundamentally sound sequence like the seance in *Miracles for Sale,* Browning's visual intuition fortifies the impact by having the spirit noises emanate from a perfectly black screen.

Most of Browning's films stick to the format of melodrama with episodes of horror, but there are at least two in which he carefully develops suspense over an extended period of time.

Nearly one half of *White Tiger* is played out in the secluded cabin where Sylvia, Hawkes and Roy have cloistered themselves following a daring jewellery heist. Each feels that the others are planning a double-cross and Roy suspects Hawkes of being the man who informed on his father. Browning emphasises this mistrust by isolating the characters in separate close-ups as they survey their partners and then, after Longworth's unexpected arrival, separating them into constantly changing groups. When Hawkes and Roy go into the bedroom to interrogate Longworth, Sylvia tries to hide some of the loot. As Sylvia and Longworth chat outdoors, Roy keeps them under surveillance from the window. Several superstitious omens—a black cat, thirteen pieces of jewellery,

THE UNHOLY THREE: tension mounts among the characters in the cabin scene (with Chaney, McLaglen, Earles, Mae Busch). Courtesy John Kobal

MARK OF THE VAMPIRE: Browning and James Wong Howe set up a shot (courtesy Films Inc., U.S.A. and M-G-M)

a broken mirror—add empirically to the mounting suspense. The claustrophobic cabin contains the action in such a way that the pressure builds to an explosive point.

Shifting permutations of mistrust have much the same effect in the cabin scene of *The Unholy Three*. Here, however, the signs of conflict and provocation are stronger. Tweedledee openly taunts Rosie, gleefully singing a song of unrequited love while manipulating Echo's grinning dummy. The gorilla feeds in his locked room and the strongman carefully cleans his shotgun. Powerfully suggestive images, like that of the dwarf eyeing McLaglen's firearm

The shot alluded to on opposite page, dominated in the film by an irridescent glow

as the pair observe Rosie and Echo in the distance, provide a visual element of stress. The tempo of the dangerous changes in allegiance accelerates until, in the precisely orchestrated finale, Hercules asks Rosie to abscond with him and attacks her when she resists. The dwarf uncages the gorilla who kills McLaglen after McLaglen strangles the dwarf. Again, the effect is one of a release of tension by an explosion of action.

Mark of the Vampire is another film that is developed without reliance upon unexpected shock. The trumped-up scheme to force a murderer to re-enact his crime is merely a construct upon which to build a compelling mood piece. The delicate, silkily evil texture obtained is as much a triumph for James Wong Howe's lighting as it is for Browning's sense of the unreal. Howe has bathed his sets in an eerie, luminous glow which is free of the harsh shadows and contrasts that mark Freund's work in *Dracula*. Freund's lighting is theatrical; Howe's is natural. Accordingly, the thrusts of the two films differ markedly. *Dracula* is pure Grand Guignol, frightening us with the prospect of becoming the vampire's victim. The menace in *Mark of the Vampire* is undefined and relates more to the other-worldly atmosphere evoked by the demonic couple rather than to specific powers they may possess. The audience is more concerned with its own uneasiness than it is with any peril that threatens the characters.

In *Dracula*, Browning clarifies some of the early action by means of one of his favourite devices, an animal montage in which a particularly sinister event is intercut with shots of small creatures. As each of Dracula's wives emerges from her tomb a rooting rat disappears behind a ledge or a wasp pulls itself from a tiny coffin-shaped compartment. The metaphor defines the nature of the vampire and conveys the impression of a rewakening of evil and a parasitic search for sustenance. On the other hand, the corresponding sequence in *Mark of the Vampire* uses the inserts to give impetus to an intricately rhythmic passage. As Bela Lugosi and the bat-girl descend the cobweb-covered staircase of the abandoned mansion, their progress is broken into a series of shots, each of which involves continuous movement of either the camera, the players or both. This creates the impression of an easy, unearthly gliding motion. By alternating these with glimpses of bats, rats and insects scurrying about, Browning provides a beat which accents the steady, deliberate progress of the horrific pair. There is no sacrifice of smoothness and the two seem to be, at once, floating and walking. The strange varieties of animals used has a bearing

DRACULA: Bela Lugosi and Dwight Frye in long shot. Gothic shadows by Karl Freund

upon establishing the unnatural atmosphere. Spiders and rats are familiar fright symbols, but one is occasionally taken aback by the sight of an armadillo lurking about the crypt. The effect is disorientation and the viewer becomes ill-at-ease because he has entered a universe that is entirely outside his realm of natural experience. This is the impact of the animal montage in *West of Zanzibar*

MARK OF THE VAMPIRE: Bela Lugosi

when alligators, giant lizards, exotic birds and jungle insects herald the march of the voodoo monster.

The religious symbolism which turns up periodically in Browning's pictures serves two antagonistic ends. When Dead Legs discovers his dead wife and her child on the pulpit of the cathedral, the solemn surroundings lend a tone of fanatical irrevocability to his vow to "make Crane and his brat pay." The altar statue of the Virgin and child attests to the innocence of his spouse and baby. At the same time, Chaney's difficult and painful movements upon his belly at the front of the church (vaguely recalling his role in *The Miracle Man*) have the look of a savage parody of a religious supplicant whose faith has been rendered a mockery. God's justice having failed, Dead Legs is about to embark upon his own mission of righteousness.

As Singapore Joe gazes longingly at his daughter through the window of the curio shop, the display of crucifixes testifies of his love for her while paradoxically acting as a barrier between them. The Black Bird/Bishop easily deceives Fifi, Bertie, the police and the locals with his phoney mantle of religious goodness. When Paul Lavond threatens the last of the bankers with a coded note, decipherable by assembling words from the Bible, the "Good Book" suddenly carries a message of effective justice. Religion for the Browning hero is, then, an additional spring of frustration—another defaulted promise.

Browning's overall contribution to the cinema is an insulated one. Many people, to be sure, have emulated the style of *Dracula* and the titles of some of the Chaney films have become legendary (more for their star than their director). Browning's work acquires its full impact only when considered cumulatively. It is only then that we begin to sense the fanaticism behind the director's pursuit of his themes of justice and frustration and his intense involvement with his monster heroes, and start to develop intuitive feelings

THE THIRTEENTH CHAIR: Lugosi as he appeared in his pre-DRACULA career

about the ferocious vision that gave rise to the audacious *Freaks* and revelled in the fantasised decapitation in *The Show*. Each newly discovered film of this talented monomaniac strengthens our impressions of the rest of his output. Browning, then, is a perfect model of the way an *auteur* approach can enhance our appreciation of the work of selected movie-makers.

Tod Browning had the good fortune to be a complete film-maker, producing and developing scenarios for many of his pictures. Without this kind of independence, *Freaks*, undoubtedly the most personal film made at M-G-M during the Thirties, would have been an impossible project. The disastrous public reaction to this film, however, seems to have shaken front office confidence in its director. In the following seven years he worked on only four pictures and, in 1944, five years after *Miracles for Sale*, "Variety" published his obituary. He actually died in 1962, one year before a screening of *Freaks* at the Venice Film Festival generated renewed interest in his unique career.

THE ROAD TO MANDALAY: Singapore Joe's daughter (Lois Moran) is surrounded by religious paraphernalia. Henry Walthall is the priest

TOD BROWNING Filmography

This filmography does not include Browning's work as an actor; he directed all the films listed here.

JIM BLUDSO (1917). Adventures of a hero on the Mississippi river who forgives an unfaithful wife and settles down with the woman who has reared his child. *Sc:* (from the poem by John Hay). *With* Wilfred Lucas (*Jim Bludso*), Winifred Westover (*Kate Taggart*), George Stone (*Little Breeches*), Charles Lee, **Monte Blue, Bert Woodruff, Lillian Lang**don, Sam de Grasse, Olga Graeme. *Prod:* Fine Arts/Triangle.

PEGGY, THE WILL O' THE WISP (1917). *Sc:* (story by Katharine Kavanaugh). *Prod:* B. A. Rolfe/Metro. 5 reels.

THE JURY OF FATE (1917). *Sc:* June **Mathis (story by Finis Fox).** *Prod:* B. A. Rolfe/Metro. 5 reels.

THE EYES OF MYSTERY (1918). Adventures of an heir in a mysterious Virginia mansion. "The House in the Mist", involving moonshiners, kidnappers, and a strange will. *Sc:* June Mathis (story "The House in the Mist" by Octavus Roy Cohen and J. U. Giesy). *Ph:* H. L. Keepers. *With* Edith Storey (*Carma*), Bradley **Barker, Harry S. Northrup.** *Prod:* B. A. Rolfe/Metro. 5 reels.

THE LEGION OF DEATH (1918). *Sc:* June Mathis (from her story). *Ph:* H. L. Keepers. *With* Edith Storey. *Prod:* Metro. 7 reels.

REVENGE (1918). *Sc:* H. P. Keeler, William Parker (the novel "Hearts Steadfast" by Edward Moffat). *Ph:* W. C.
60

Thompson. *With* Edith Storey. *Prod:* Metro. 7 reels.

WHICH WOMAN (1918). Comedy-drama in which an amateur chauffeur and a runaway bride get the better of a band of burglars. *Sc:* Anthony W. Coldeway (the novel by Evelyn Campbell). *Ph:* John Brown. *With* Ella Hall, Priscilla Dean, Edward Johnson, Andrew Robson. *Prod:* Bluebird Photoplays. 5 reels.

THE DECIDING KISS (1918) Four unmarried members of society adopt a child of sixteen; the two men in the group fall in love with her much to the jealousy of the two women. *Sc:* Bernard McConville (the novel by Ethel M. Kelly). *Ph:* John Brown. *With* Edith Roberts, William Cartwright, William Lloyd, Mrs. Clair, Winifred Greenwood, Lottie Cruze. *Prod:* Bluebird. 5 reels.

THE BRAZEN BEAUTY (1918). A self-willed young woman achieves wealth and **fame but happiness long eludes her.** *Sc:* William E. Wing (story by Louise Winters). *With* Priscilla Dean (*Jacala Averill*). *Prod:* Bluebird. 5 reels.

SET FREE (1918). *Sc:* Tod Browning (story by Joseph Franklin Poland). *With* Edith Roberts. *Prod:* Bluebird. 5 reels.

THE WICKED DARLING (1919). Romantic melodrama concerning a beautiful young jewel thief. *Sc:* Harvey Gates (story by Evelyn Campbell). *With* Priscilla Dean (*Mary Stevens*), Lon Chaney **(*Stoop*), Wellington Playter (*Kent Morti-*** *mer*), Spottiswood Aitken (*Fanem*), Gertrude Astor (*Adele Hoyt*). *Prod:* Universal. 6 reels.

THE EXQUISITE THIEF (1919). *Sc:* Harvey Gates (story "Raggedy Ann" by Charles W. Tyler). *With* Priscilla Dean. *Prod:* Universal. 6 reels.

THE UNPAINTED WOMAN (1919). *Sc:* Waldemar Young (story by Sinclair Lewis). *With* Mary MacLaren. *Prod:* Universal. 6 reels.

A PETAL ON THE CURRENT (1919). *Sc:* Waldemar Young (story by Fannie Hunt). *With* Mary MacLaren. *Prod:* Universal. 6 reels.

BONNIE, BONNIE LASSIE (1919). A girl leaves Scotland for America and becomes the assistant to a signboard painter with whom she falls in love. *Sc:* Tod Browning, Violet Clark (story by Henry C. Rowland). *With* Mary MacLaren (*Ailsa Graeme*), Spottiswood Aitken, David Butler. *Prod:* Universal. 6 reels.

THE VIRGIN OF STAMBOUL (1920). Spectacular melodrama of a Turk who fancies a virgin beggar girl as an addition to his harem but loses her through the intervention of an American who loves her. *Sc:* Tod Browning, William Parker (story by H. H. Van Loan). *With* Priscilla Dean (*Sari*), Wallace Beery (*Achmet Hamid*), Wheeler Oakman (*Capt. Carlisle Pemberton*). *Prod:* Universal (Jewel). 7 reels.

OUTSIDE THE LAW (1921). A safecracker and his girlfriend/partner refuse to split their take with Black Mike Sylva, head of the mob. *Sc:* Lucien Hubbard and Browning (story by Browning). *Ph:* William Fildew. *With* Priscilla Dean (*Molly Madden*), Ralph Lewis (*Silent Madden*), Lon Chaney (*Black Mike Silva* and *Ah Wing*), Wheeler Oakman, E. A. Warren, Stanley Goethals, Melbourne MacDowell, Wilton Taylor. *Prod:* Universal (Jewel). 8 reels.

NO WOMAN KNOWS (1921). Woman is caught in conflict between appeal of a family life and success in the business world. *Sc:* Browning and George Yohalem (the novel "Fanny Herself" by Edna Ferber). *Ph:* William Fildew. *With* Max Davidson (*F. Brandeis*), Snitz Edwards (*Herr Bauer*), Grace Marvin (*Molly Brandeis*), E. A. Warren (*Rabbi Thalman*), Bernice Radom (*Fanny*), Raymond Lee, Joseph Swickard, Richard Cummings, Joseph Sterns, Mabel Julienne Scott, John Davidson, Earl Schenck, Stuart Holmes. *Prod:* Universal (Jewel). 7 reels.

THE WISE KID (1922). Girl sees through slick suitor and abandons him for honest baker. *Sc:* Wallace Clifton (story by William Slavens McNutt). *Ph:* William Fildew. *With* Gladys Walton (*Rosie Cooper*), David Butler (*Freddie Smith*), Hallam Cooley (*Harry*), Hector Sarno, Henry A. Barrows, C. Norman Hammond. *Prod:* Universal. 5 reels.

UNDER TWO FLAGS (1922). A French-Arab girl clears her lover in the French Foreign Legion of a charge of treason, then dies stopping the execution. *Sc:* Edward T. Lowe and Elliot Clawson (adaptation by Browning and Edward Lowe Jr. of the book by "Ouida"). *Ph:* William Fildew. *With* Priscilla Dean (*Cigarette*), James Kirkwood (*Corporal Victor*), John Davidson (*Sheik Ben Ali Hammad*), Stuart Holmes, Ethyl Grey Terry, Robert Mack, Burton Law, Albert Pollet, W. H. Bainbridge. *Prod:* Universal. 8 reels.

MAN UNDER COVER (1922). A young man saves a town from a con man's swindle with a swindle of his own. *Sc:*

Harvey Gates (story by L. V. Eyetinge). *Ph:* Virgil Miller. *With* Herbert Rawlinson (*Paul Porter*), George Hernandez (*Daddy Moffat*), Wm. Courtwright (*Mayor Harper*), George Webb, Edwin Booth Tilton, Gerald Pring, Barbara Bedford, Willis Marks. *Prod:* Universal. 5 reels.

DRIFTING (1923). American girl smuggles opium and falls in love with the undercover agent she plots to kill. *Sc:* Browning and A. P. Younger (the novel "Drifting" by John Colton and Daisy Andrews). *Ph:* William Fildew. *Ed:* Errol Taggart. *With* Priscilla Dean (*Cassie Cook/Lucille Preston*), Matt Moore (*Capt. Jarvis*), Wallace Beery (*Jules Repin*), Anna May Wong (*Rose Li*), J. Farrell MacDonald, Rose Dione, Edna Tichenor, Wm. V. Mong. *Prod:* Universal (Jewel). 7 reels.

WHITE TIGER (1923). Young gangster seeks revenge for the murder of his father. The man responsible for the death is the partner of the boy's love. The trio execute a jewel heist. *Sc:* Browning and Charles Kenyon (story by Browning). *Ph:* Wm. Fildew. With Priscilla Dean (*Sylvia Donovan*), Matt Moore (*Longworth*), Raymond Griffith (*Roy Donovan*), Wallace Beery (*Hawkes*). *Prod:* Universal (Jewel). 7 reels.

DAY OF FAITH (1923). The attempt of selfish millionaire to break up an affair between his son and a female missionhouse keeper leads to the son's death. The wealthy man turns into a social reformer. *Sc:* June Mathis and Katharine Kavanaugh (the book "The Day of Faith" by Arthur Somers Roche). *Ph:* William Fildew. *With* Eleanor Boardman (*Jane Maynard*), Tyrone Power (*Michael An-*

stell), Raymond Griffith (*Tom Barnett*), Wallace MacDonald (*John Anstell*), Ford Sterling (*Montreal Sammy*), Charles Conklin (*Yeggs Darby*), Ruby Lafayette, Jane Mercer, Edw. Martindel, Winter Hall, Emmett King, Jack Curtis, Fredrick Vroom, John Curry, Henry Herbert, Myles McCarthy. *Prod:* Goldwyn Pictures for Goldwyn-Cosmopolitan. 7 reels.

THE DANGEROUS FLIRT (1924). After an innocent scandal, a girl's puritanical upbringing threatens to destroy her marriage and involves her in Latin American intrigue. *Sc:* E. Richard Schayer (from "The Prude" by Julie Herne). *Ph:* Lucien Andriot and Maynard Rugg. *Cast:* Evelyn Brent (*Sheila Fairfax*), Edward Earle (*Dick Morris*), Sheldon Lewis (*Don Alfonso*), Clarissa Selwynne, Pierre Gendron. *Prod:* Gothic for FBO. 6 reels.

SILK STOCKING SAL (1924). A reformed female gangster saves her boyfriend from a murder rap by tricking a confession from a gangster chieftain. *Sc:* **E. Richard Schayer. *Ph:* Silvano Balboni.** *With* Evelyn Brent (*"Stormy" Martin*), Robert Ellis (*Bob Cooper*), Earl Metcalfe, Alice Browning, Virginia Madison, Louis Fitzroy, John Gough. *Prod:* Gothic for FBO. 5 reels.

THE UNHOLY THREE (1925). Jewellery theft ring cases prospective robbery sites by **disguising ventriloquist as old** lady and dwarf as a baby. Their attempt to frame a pet store clerk with a murder charge fails when the ventriloquist has a change of heart. *Sc:* Waldemar Young (story "The Unholy Three" by Tod Robbins). *Ph:* David Kesson. *Art dir:* Cedric Gibbons and Joseph Wright. *Ed:* Daniel Gray. *With* Lon Chaney (*Echo*), Mae Busch (*Rosie*), Matt Moore (*Hector Mac-*

Donald), Victor McLaglen (*Hercules*), Harry Earles (*Tweedledee*), Harry Betz (*Regan*), Edward Connelly, William Humphreys, A. E. Warren, John Merkyl, Charles Wellesley. *Prod:* Browning for M-G-M. 7 reels. Currently available in USA (16mm) through Films, Inc.

THE MYSTIC (1925). Gangster uses gypsy seance to con heiress. He reforms and falls in love with one of the gypsies. *Sc:* Waldemar Young (a story by Browning). *Ph:* Ira Morgan. *Art dir:* Cedric Gibbons and Harvey Libbert. *Ed:* Frank Sullivan. *With* Aileen Pringle (*Zara*), Conway Tearle (*Michael Nash*), Mitchell Lewis (*Zazarack*), Robert Ober (*Anton*), Stanton Heck, David Torrence, Gladys Hulette, DeWitt Jennings. *Prod:* M-G-M. 7 reels.

DOLLAR DOWN (1925). Manoeuvres in high finance. When a girl and her mother fall prey to installment sharks, she becomes inadvertently involved in a land speculation deal. *Sc:* Fred Stowers (a story by Jane Courthope and Ethel Hill). *Ph:* Allen Thompson. *With* Ruth Roland (*Ruth Craig*), Henry B. Walthall (*Alec Craig*), Maym Kelso (*Mrs. Craig*), Earl Schenck (*Grant Elliott*), Claire McDowell, Roscoe Karns. *Prod:* Co-Artists for Truart. 6 reels.

THE BLACK BIRD (1926). The gangster chief of London's Limehouse district evades the law by assuming the identity of a crippled clergyman. He attempts to turn two lovers—a wealthy con man and a French cabaret singer—against each other. *Sc:* Waldemar Young (story by Browning). *Ph:* Percy Hilburn. *Art dir:* Cedric Gibbons and Arnold Gillespie. *Ed:* Errol Taggart. *With* Lon Chaney (*Dan Tate*), René Adorée (*Fifi*), Doris Lloyd

(*Polly*), Owen Moore (*Bertie*), Lionel Belmore. *Prod:* M-G-M. 7 reels. Currently available in USA (16mm) through Films, Inc.

THE ROAD TO MANDALAY (1926). Singapore gangster struggles to prevent the marriage of his daughter to one of his smuggling colleagues. *Sc:* Elliott Clawson (story by Browning and Herman Mankiewicz). *Ph:* Merritt Gerstad. *Art dir:* Cedric Gibbons and Arnold Gillespie. *Ed:* Errol Taggart. *With* Lon Chaney (*Singapore Joe*), Lois Moran (*Joe's daughter*), Owen Moore (*The Admiral*), Henry B. Walthall (*Father James*), Kamiyama Sojin (*English Charlie Wing*), John George (*Servant*). *Prod:* M-G-M. 7 reels.

LONDON AFTER MIDNIGHT (1927). A hypnotist uses a vampire masquerade to make a murderer confess. *Sc:* Waldemar Young (story by Browning). *Ph:* Merritt Gerstad. *Art dir:* Cedric Gibbons and Arnold Gillespie. *Ed:* Harry Reynolds. *With* Lon Chaney (*Burke*), Marceline Day (*Lucille Balfour*), Henry B. Walthall (*Sir James Hamlin*), Percy Williams, Conrad Nagel, Polly Moran. *Prod:* M-G-M. 7 reels.

THE SHOW (1927) A jealous quarrel against a carnival background results in several murders and attempted murders. *Sc:* Waldemar Young (novel "The Day of Souls" by Charles Tenny Jackson). *Ph:* John Arnold. *Art dir:* Cedric Gibbons and Richard Day. *Ed:* Errol Taggart. *With* John Gilbert (*Cock Robin*), Renée Adorée (*Salome*), Lionel Barrymore (*The Greek*), Edward Connelly, Gertrude Short. *Prod:* M-G-M. 7 reels. Currently available in USA (16mm) through Films, Inc.

THE UNKNOWN (1927) Alonzo The

THE BIG CITY: Chaney, without make-up in a characteristic gangster role (courtesy Films Inc., and M-G-M)

Armless Wonder strangles the circus owner and then has his arms amputated to be free from suspicion and to retain the love of the owner's neurotic daughter. *Sc:* Waldemar Young (story by Browning). *Ph:* Merritt Gerstad. *Art dir:* Cedric Gibbons and Richard Day. *Ed:* Harry Reynolds, Errol Taggart. *With* Lon Chaney (*Alonzo*), Norman Kerry (*Malabar*), Joan Crawford (*Estrellita*), Nick de Ruiz (*Zanzi*), John George (*Cojo*). *Prod:* M-G-M. 6 reels.

THE BIG CITY (1928). Gangster uses costume jewellery store as front for his jewel theft operation. After a conflict with a rival gang, he and his girl-friend
64

reform. *Sc:* Waldemar Young (story by Browning). *Ph:* Henry Sharp. *Art dir:* Cedric Gibbons. *Ed:* Henry Reynolds. *With* Lon Chaney (*Chuck*), Marceline Day (*Sunshine*), James Murray (*Curly*), Betty Compson (*Helen*), John George (*The Arab*), Walter Percival. *Prod:* Browning for M-G-M. 7 reels

WEST OF ZANZIBAR (1928). A circus performer, crippled when his wife's lover pushes him from a balcony, follows his enemy to the heart of Africa where he plots a macabre revenge. *Sc:* Elliott Clawson, Waldemar Young (story by Chester De Vonde and Kilbourne Gordon). *Ph:* Percy Hilburn. *Art dir:* Cedric Gibbons. *Ed:* Harry Reynolds. *With* Lon Chaney (*Dead Legs*), Lionel Barrymore (*Crane*), Mary Nolan (*Daughter*), Warner Baxter (*Doctor*), Roscoe Ward (*Tiny*), Kalla Pasha (*Babe*). *Prod:* M-G-M. 7 reels. Currently available in USA (16mm) through Films, Inc.

WHERE EAST IS EAST (1929). The daughter of an Asian trapper is to be wed to the son of a circus owner. The girl's mother attempts to steal the prospective bridegroom from her daughter, prompting the father to take drastic steps. *Sc:* Waldemar Young, Richard Schayer (story by Browning and Harry Sinclair Drago). *Ph:* Henry Sharp. *Art dir:* Cedric Gibbons. *Ed:* Harry Reynolds. *With* Lon Chaney (*Tiger Haynes*), Lupe Velez (*Toyo*), Estelle Taylor (*M. de Silva*), Lloyd Hughes (*Bobby Bailey*), Louis Stern. *Prod:* Browning for M-G-M. 7 reels. Currently available in USA (16mm) through Films, Inc.

THE THIRTEENTH CHAIR (1929). A reconstruction of a fatal seance is used to trap a murderer. *Sc:* Elliott Clawson.

Ph: Merritt B. Gerstad. *Ed:* Harry Reynolds. *Art dir:* Cedric Gibbons. *With* Conrad Nagel (*Richard Crosby*), Leila Hyams (*Helen O'Neill*), Margaret Wycherly (*Madame LaGrange*), Helene Miliard (*Mary Eastwood*), Holmes Herbert (*Sir Roscoe Crosby*), Mary Forbes, Bela Lugosi. *Prod:* Browning for M-G-M. 8 reels (sound). (Released in both sound and silent versions.)

OUTSIDE THE LAW (1930). Re-make of Browning's 1921 silent. *Sc:* Browning and Garrett Fort. *Ph:* Roy Overbaugh. *Mus:* David Broekman. *Art dir:* William Schmidt. *Ed:* Milton Carruth. *With* Mary Nolan (*Connie*), Edward G. Robinson (*Cobra*), Owen Moore (*Fingers O'Dell*), Edwin Sturgis (*Jake*), John George (*Humpy*), Delmar Watson (*The Kid*), DeWitt Jennings (*Police captain*), Rockcliffe Fellows (*O'Reilly*), Frank Burke, Sidney Bracey. *Prod:* E. M. Asher for Universal. 81m.

DRACULA (1931). Classic story of the hunt for a Transylvanian vampire in London. *Sc:* Garrett Fort (the novel by Bram Stoker and the play by Hamilton Deane and John L. Balderston). *Ph:* Karl Freund. *With* Bela Lugosi (*Dracula*), Helen Chandler (*Mina*), Dwight Frye (*Renfield*), David Manners (*Harker*), Edward Van Sloan (*Van Helsing*), Frances Dade, Herbert Bunston. *Prod:* Universal. 85m. Currently available in USA (16mm) through Universal 16.

THE IRON MAN (1931). A prizefighter is in a constant squeeze between his manager and his wife. *Sc:* Francis Edward Faragoh (a novel by W. R. Burnett). *Ph:* Percy Hilburn. *Ed:* Milton Carruth. *With* Lew Ayres (*Young Mason*), Robert Armstrong (*Regan*), Jean

Harlow (*Rose*), John Miljan (*Lewis*), Mike Donlim (*McNeil*), Morrie Cohan, Mary Doran, Mildred Van Dorn, Ned Sparks, Sam Blum, Sammy Gervon. *Prod:* Carl Laemmle Jr. for Universal. 73m.

FREAKS (1932). A colony of circus freaks avenges a dwarf who is victimised by a beautiful trapeze artiste and her strongman boyfriend. *Sc:* Willis Goldbeck and Leon Gordon (the short story "Spurs" by Tod Robbins). *Ph:* Merritt Gerstad. *Ed:* Basil Wrangell. *With* Wallace Ford (*Phroso*), Leila Hyams (*Venus*), Olga Baclanova (*Cleopatra*), Henry Victor (*Hercules*), Harry Earles (*Hans*), Daisy Earles (*Frieda*), Daisy and Violet Hilton (*The Siamese Twins*), Rose Dion, Edward Brophy, Matt McHugh, Randian, Johnny Eck, Martha the Armless Wonder. *Prod:* Browning for M-G-M. 90m.

FAST WORKERS (1933). A construction worker tries to prove to his pal that the girl he plans to marry is a "gold-digger." *Sc:* Carl Brown, Ralph Wheelwright, Laurence Stallings (the play "Rivets" by John McDermot). *Ph:* Peverell Marley. *Art dir:* Cedric Gibbons. *Ed:* Ben Lewis. *With* John Gilbert (*Gunner Smith*), Robert Armstrong (*Bucker Reilly*), Mae Clarke (*Mary*), Muriel Kirkland (*Millie*), Vince Barnett (*Spike*), Virginia Cherrill (*Virginia*), Muriel Evans (*Nurse*), Sterling Holloway (*Pinky Magoo*), Guy Usher (*Scudder*), Warner Richmond (*Feets Wilson*), Robert Burns (*Alabam'*). *Prod:* Browning for M-G-M. 68m.

MARK OF THE VAMPIRE (1935). Re-make of *London After Midnight.* *Sc:* Guy Endore and Bernard Schubert. *Ph:* James Wong Howe. *Ed:* Ben Lewis. *With* Lionel Barrymore (*Prof. Zelen*), Elizabeth Allan

65

(*Irena Borotyn*), Bela Lugosi (*Count Mora*), Lionel Atwill (*Inspector Neumann*), Jean Hersholt (*Murderer*), Holmes Herbert (*Sir Karell Borotyn*), Donald Meek (*Dr. Doskill*), Henry Wadsworth, Jessie Ralph, Carol Borland (*Luna*). *Prod:* M-G-M. 60m. Currently available in USA (16mm) through Films, Inc.

THE DEVIL-DOLL (1936). A man escaped from prison uses miniature human beings to avenge himself upon the men who framed him. *Sc:* Browning, Garrett Fort, Guy Endore and Erich Von Stroheim (from the novel "Burn, Witch Burn" by Abraham Merritt). *Ph:* Leonard Smith. *Ed:* Frederick Smith. *With* Lionel Barrymore (*Paul Lavond*), Maureen O'Sullivan (*Lorraine, Lavond's daughter*), Frank Lawton, Henry B. Walthall, Rafaela Ottiano, Grace Ford, Arthur Hohl, Juanita Quigley, Lucy Beaumont, Robert Greig, Pedro de Cordoba. *Prod:* Edgar Mannix for M-G-M. 79m. Currently available in USA (16mm) through Films, Inc.

MIRACLES FOR SALE (1939). Murder mystery among practitioners of the occult. The case is solved by a purveyor of magic show equipment. *Sc:* Harry Ruskin, Marion Parsonnet, and James Edward Grant (the novel "Death from a Top Hat" by Clayton Rawson). *Ph:* Charles Lawton. *Art dir:* Edwin B. Willis and Cedric Gibbons. *Ed:* Fredrick Smith. *With* Robert Young (*Michael Morgan*), Florence Rice (*Judy Barkley*), Frank Craven (*Dad Morgan*), Lee Bowman (*La Clair*), Henry Hull (*Frank Duvallo*), Astrid Allwyn (*Mrs. LaClair*), Cliff Clark (*Inspector*), Walter Kingsford (*Cal Watrous*), Frederic Worlock (*Dr. Sabbat*), Gloria Holden, William Demarest, Harold Monjin. *Prod:* M-G-M. 71m.

Acknowledgements (Browning)

I am deeply indebted to many people without whose help this study would have been impossible. Doug Lemza, Al Green and Frank Pedi were especially helpful in arranging screenings from the Films, Inc. library and in supplying stills. Kevin Brownlow's screenings, stills (with John Kobal) and advice were also crucial to the completion of the study. Other, equally important screenings and stills were provided by Gary Johnson at M-G-M, St. Louis; and Bill Blair of United Films, Tulsa. Further vital assistance was rendered by George Fasel who read the manuscript and made many valuable suggestions and by Jane Winter who devoted much valuable time to typing the manuscript. Finally, I must acknowledge the influence of Eliot Feldman and the Dwight Frye Fan Club for arousing my interest in the work of Tod Browning.

Don Siegel

Director Don Siegel and his films are important subjects for research and study because his continuing exploration of certain themes within his work, allied with his concern for his craft, give his career a historical uniqueness in terms of the Hollywood studio film.

Siegel was born in Chicago on October 26, 1912. He grew up surrounded by accomplished elders and peers, who gave him every opportunity to follow his inclinations in choosing a career. He passed his exam at Cambridge (England), lived for a while in Paris and arrived penniless in California in 1934. There he contacted an uncle who put him in touch with Hal Wallis at Warner Bros. Wallis got him started as a film librarian. From that post he became an assistant editor and later moved into the insert department. Of this job Siegel has said, "I took it out of boredom and curiosity. Then for the first time I found myself in love with the movies."[1] Working under the then head of special effects, Byron Haskin, Siegel eventually set up the montage department and the style of his films evolved from that period. Montages rapidly advance the story through a succession of overlapping or dissolving clips and cross-cutting. During this time (1939–45) he also did second units for the studio.

After a run-in with the head of the studio, Jack Warner, over whether or not he should be given the chance, Siegel began directing with two shorts, *Star in the Night* and *Hitler Lives?* (1945) which both won Academy Awards. In his first feature, *The Verdict* (1946), he deliberately avoided the use of montage, but years of creating montages had been irrevocably stamped upon his style and there are few films which do not display the editing techniques he developed then.

Don Siegel's films reflect his rage at feeling powerless to deal with the real world—the universe beyond film-making. His movies are an exorcism of personal furies, worked out against the regulated madness of contemporary urban America. Their famous energy and violence are American to the core and give vent to the anger and pessimism which are at the heart of all his films. Siegel is caught between his dynamic wrath and the force which produces it—his frustration with the world.

This study will focus on some of the most important elements in Siegel's cinema:

1. The emergence of the American anti-hero and the thin line between hero and anti-hero
2. The damaged vulnerable hero
3. Sex and the strong or fatal woman
4. Pessimism
5. Limitations of time (characters reach a dead-end)
6. Original assumptions, convictions turned against the protagonist
7. Dynamism and fate
8. What is the source of danger and where does help come from?

Dirty Harry (1971) portrays Clint Eastwood as the prototypical, thwarted Siegel anti-hero. Harry, the police detective (Eastwood), is at war, not only with crime and its perpetrators, but with the society which allows the criminal so much freedom and restricts the law, making an inhospitable *milieu* in which to indulge his inclinations to administer justice on the spot. Harry is Siegel, seething behind steely blue eyes and throwing his badge into the swamp where the Scorpio killer's body has just fallen. Harry's attitude is that if living by the book means coddling scum, the city will have to survive without his help.

Many of the heroes of Siegel's films—Madigan and Coogan—

Siegel talks over a point on CHARLEY VARRICK with Walter Matthau

like Harry, do not possess the flexibility to escape from the situations in which they find themselves locked. It's not clear that they want to break out; they seem to relish their predicaments and view them as opportunities for perverse achievement, giving them the scope in which to indulge their well-developed, if subconscious, cruelty.

Thus Siegel (his heroes are almost indistinguishable from his anti-heroes: there is little variation in the men Eastwood portrays in *Coogan's Bluff* [1969], *The Beguiled* [1971] and in his unconventional hero, Harry) shows his disappointment with the world through these protagonists—not as a depressive, but as a virile force, expressed through and countered by the dynamism of these men. Almost all of Siegel's films after 1960 have basically the same hero: the potent, super-masculine, irresistible force, struggling through oppressive turmoil to reach his goals.

This view comes from the traditions of early American movies as exemplified by the films of D. W. Griffith. In Griffith's highly personal cinema the issues are clear-cut and resolution of the conflict is carried out single-mindedly by a truly heroic, but battered warrior/knight. Life was simpler for Griffith. His heroes were not bothered by problems of conscience or ethics, by remorse, doubt or guilt, and were tangibly rewarded by the love of a good woman, the adulation of their peers or the respect of their elders. These honourable men plunged into the fray and did what needed doing. In the words of Lee J. Cobb to Eastwood's Coogan, "A man's gotta do what a man's gotta do." Their goals were nobler and their triumphs undirtied by bodies strewn in their wake, but they were essentially the forebears of Harry, Madigan and Coogan. This is not to assume that Siegel would have been happier making films in 1920. His conflicts are inward, personal, and his movies are an attempt to resolve them on the screen.

The limitations placed upon him by the material he is given to film are sometimes severe and he circumvents them with agility and grace. However, the plot points which he is unable to resolve are quite noticeable: for instance, Eastwood's inability to see that the tide has turned and that the women in *The Beguiled* are scheming against him. We are here asked to accept the fact that the Eastwood character is so dense and conceited that he can't see what is happening, when previously we have seen him sidestep moral and logistical issues with considerable deftness. The black-and-white terms, the sharply defined heroes and villains of Griffith's time have been transformed into the confused and ambiguous characters who people the dirty underbelly of the straight world in Siegel's films. The frustrations evident in Siegel himself and expressed through his heroes and anti-heroes give his films their motivating intensity.

The structure and essence of Siegel's movies vary little from film to film. The picture begins with either an explosion of emotional and physical force onto the screen (*Madigan,* [1968], *The Killers* [1964]), or a slow build-up (*Hell Is for Heroes* [1962], *The Hanged Man* [1964]), both of which soon present the world portrayed as having gone askew in some vital facet. There is frequently a breakdown in the all-important organisations (criminal or police), often ending in a chase; the most interesting variation to

Action in MADIGAN, with Richard Widmark (right)

71

date being the sick plane and car ballet in *Charley Varrick* (1973). These films are direct and energetic. Siegel is impatient with exposition. The closest any Siegel film has come to displaying studio heavy-footedness (like the psychiatrist's explanation at the end of *Psycho*) occurs in the "framing" story tacked onto *Invasion of the Body Snatchers* (1956) by Allied Artists.

There is usually a criminal or police pair (*Killers,* both in *The Line-up* [1958]), sometimes functioning as mentor and student, who are separated through an argument or death. This two-headed protagonist was extended into Siegel's film about women, *The Beguiled,* in which Geraldine Page collaborated with her pupils in the demise of Eastwood.

As have D. W. Griffith's, so will some of Don Siegel's films date, particularly those which are specific in attitudes and *mores*— but they will always be respected for their dynamism, punch and brevity. His films will be studied for their structural relationship to each other and to those of other directors: Fritz Lang and Siegel share a perspective of sociological pessimism, although Siegel is more ironic and distant. They will also be examined for their view of an era through which we are now living but which will soon be grist for history's mill.

One fact which is relevant to any claims of auteurism on Siegel's behalf is the degree of control he is able to exercise in his work. Those films, like *Two Mules for Sister Sara* (1970), which bear his personal stamp in spite of studio interference are triumphs of cunning and perseverance. Siegel: "Marty Rackin [the producer] and I didn't get along. I'd make my points, but he would walk away saying 'I lose the battles, but win the war.'" The war he won on *Sara* was that "he, not I, did the final editing. It's a limited victory, because if you cut the picture in the camera, shoot the minimum . . . there isn't much leeway in editing the picture unless the producer orders more film shot."[2]

Shirley MacLaine in TWO MULES FOR SISTER SARA

Siegel (centre) shooting THE BLACK WINDMILL

Siegel had almost complete control of *Invasion, Baby Face Nelson* (1957), *Line-up* (1958), *Riot in Cell Block 11* (1954), *Flaming Star* (1960), *Hell Is for Heroes, The Killers* (1964), *Coogan's Bluff* (1969), *Beguiled* and *Harry*. In most cases his working on the script insured that his touch would everywhere be evident. He has the same artistic freedom on his most recent films, *Varrick* and *The Black Windmill* (1974).

Because he received no further offers to make feature films,

Siegel in 1961 began directing for television, working particularly on pilots which were so successful that they were all sold later as series. During 1961, '62 and '63 he directed various episodes for different series and became the producer for "The Legend of Jesse James," which ran from 1965–67. He took time out to make *Heroes* and in 1964 directed a feature for Universal, *The Killers,* the first movie made expressly for television. The film was released to theatres because its violence was thought too strong for TV in the wake of the recent Kennedy assassination. Siegel also made *The Hanged Man* and *Stranger on the Run* (1967) as television movies, and again returned to directing features with *Madigan* (1968) at Universal, where he has remained as an independent producer/director (except for his loan-out to Warner Bros. where he made *Harry*). In 1972 he signed a new contract with Universal which gives him the right to place his name above the title and to make "outside" pictures, also with his name to the fore.

Because he has been given, in many cases, larger budgets, longer shooting schedules, bigger stars and more control over the material to be filmed, his movies from 1960 on have shown the constancy of Siegel's preoccupations. His interest in the other side of normal, or visible, society; the workings of the law and the ways it oversteps its authority; the neurotic anti-hero and the treachery of women, are some of the more common *motifs* which appear in his films.

★ ★ ★

The damaged, vulnerable hero and the anti-hero are facets of the same persona and cannot be separated, even when the harm is physical as in *Duel at Silver Creek* (1952). The issue of vulnerability, of the complementary nature of good and evil, is central to a comprehension of Siegel's films.

The Verdict asks who of the three men is a hero: the vain and ambitious George Coulouris, the wronged and vindictive Sidney

75

THE BIG STEAL: Jane Greer and Robert Mitchum

Greenstreet or the fatuous Peter Lorre? Which one is not damaged, thus assailable? In *Night unto Night* (1949) Ronald Reagan is an epileptic, resigned to his fate, yet redeemed in spite of himself by Viveca Lindfors, herself threatened by the memory of her dead husband. Stephen McNally's gun arm is hurt in *Duel* and he must depend upon Audie Murphy (ludicrously attired in black leather, like a western *Wild One*), for support. McNally's ability to function is also impaired by another Siegel favourite, the Fatal Woman (in this case, Faith Domergue).

The writers of *The Big Steal* (1949) appear to have been undecided as to whether or not Robert Mitchum was to be a hero until he arrived on the set. Of this film Siegel said, "Naturally my attitude towards the picture had to be one of fun because I didn't take the story and whole situation seriously. Mitchum in the picture would come running into a sequence and the trees would be green and Bendix would be right on his heel and the trees would be bare [there was a three month gap between filming the two men as Mitchum was in jail during the initial shooting]."[3] Apparently the writers were also unable to decide if they were doing a comedy or an adventure and the film falls squarely in the middle. We are confused about Mitchum's motives until the final chase and denouement.

The anti-heroes of *Hell Is for Heroes* and *Baby Face Nelson* are psychotics. In the former, the sullen loner (Steve McQueen), though less obviously mad, sees nothing worth living for beyond his war-time environment. Having found the only home he will ever know in the Army, he effectively commits suicide during an assault on a German pillbox. Similarly, Mickey Rooney as *Baby Face Nelson,* knows that time has run out and asks his girl friend to finish him off, dying appropriately in a graveyard, his lifeblood leaking away. Mentally crippled by his small stature, he over-compensates venomously, relishing the deaths of enemies and cohorts for which he is responsible. However, no attempt is made to explain these men's behaviour in terms of either an unjust society or a cruel environment. The closest Siegel comes to allowing a verbal justification occurs in *The Line-up*. In Robert Keith's words, "Crime is aggressive. So's the law. You don't understand the criminal's need for violence."

Elvis Presley is spurned by white society and the girl he admires because he is a Kiowa in *Flaming Star* (1960); it is his colour therefore which renders him vulnerable. Robert Culp is undermined by his ignorance of the facts and by his faith in the deceitful Vera Miles, almost literally becoming *The Hanged Man*. Another (Edmond O'Brien) is done in by a frailty common to many of Siegel's leaders, pride. Richard Widmark in both *Madigan* and *Death of a Gunfighter* (1969) and Clint Eastwood in *Coogan's Bluff* and *The Beguiled* are crushed by the sin of pride; in Widmark's case, both times fatally. As Madigan, Widmark and his partner (Harry Guardino), both detectives, use their free time to help another precinct corner a known criminal (Steve Ihnat) who later proves to be wanted for murder. In the process of arrest, Ihnat takes their guns, and to compound Widmark's guilt Ihnat later uses Widmark's gun to kill a patrolman. Widmark is also related to Steve McQueen in *Heroes* in that both are fighting a losing battle with the insane, uncontrollable sides of their natures. Widmark's is more covert and contained, and his behaviour is softened in juxtaposition with that of Guardino and in contrast to the obviously mad Ihnat. The violence with which Widmark assaults Ihnat's door in both the opening and closing sequences, his fanatical insistence on being first through the door (basing his claim on two days' seniority over Guardino) and thus to die, are clear indications of his lack of balance.

Gunfighter presents Widmark as an ageing sheriff who suffers from his town's lack of trust and from his own reputation for be-

Richard Widmark and Lena Horne in DEATH OF A GUNFIGHTER

ing quick on the draw. Interestingly, (Siegel took over direction in the middle of shooting[4]), this is a rare example of the hero being given a societal role against which to work out his destiny. He has failed to keep up with the times and is damned as an anachronism, an especially painful one as he knows where the community's skeletons are buried. Widmark's pride is his belief that he can continue as usual, making no concessions to others' demands nor to the changed times.

Laid in New York and the Civil War South respectively, both *Coogan's Bluff* and *The Beguiled* present Clint Eastwood in hostile territory. As Coogan, the twentieth-century personification of

79

COOGAN'S BLUFF: Clint Eastwood and David F. Doyle

nineteenth-century values and ethics, he strides through the urban landscape, breaking rules and offending those upon whom he depends for help. Lee J. Cobb, as a Lieutenant, into whose domain he stalks, tells Eastwood angrily, his slimy cigar clenched between his teeth, that "We've got a system. Not much, but we're fond of it." Like Madigan, Eastwood loses both his gun (to thugs) and his prisoner, and like Madigan he mistreats those with whom he comes in contact: he shackles a half-naked Indian prisoner to a porch while he makes love to someone else's wife. (This occurs in the opening, Arizona, sequence and is an example of how Siegel establishes character early in a film). *The Beguiled* depicts Eastwood, like the only rooster in a henhouse, flaunting his sexuality in the faces of several frustrated women who eventually pay him back, first by confining him behind boarded windows, then by amputating his leg, and lastly by killing him.

In *Private Hell 36* (1954) Steve Cochran is sexually vulnerable in a way different to Eastwood. Lured by Ida Lupino's frank gold-digger, he steals $80,000 and proposes escaping to Mexico with her. In *Invasion of the Body Snatchers* Kevin McCarthy is assailable through his capacity for trust and in his need for love. If he hadn't trusted Larry Gates, speaking as the voice of wisdom and temperance, he would have left town sooner and wouldn't have ended up on the highway screaming in terror and desperation.

Audie Murphy compromises his ethics to become one of *The Gun Runners* (1958), and in the insignificant *An Annapolis Story* (1955) John Derek is injured and cannot accompany his brother on their summer training cruise before graduating from naval school.

Henry Fonda, as the *Stranger on the Run,* is a drunk, crippled by what he believes are his past sins. He is as cursed by his need for liquor as the railroad sheriff (Michael Parks) is by his need to kill. "You've come to like it, haven't you? You've come to need it," his partner (Dan Duryea) tells Parks who walks a tight-rope between normality and insanity—a condition Siegel's conception of the town reinforces through its dry, dusty landscape, the tumbleweed, and air of general hopelessness.

Because he's behind bars in *Riot in Cell Block 11,* Neville Brand is subject to the vindictive authorities who threaten to add thirty years to his sentence for leading the insurrection. However, the film makes a case for him as a hero, because he acted through unselfish motives, unlike his fellow convict (Leo Gordon) who embodies the familiar psychopathic inclinations of many Siegel protagonists. These two are the criminal counterparts of the Widmark/Guardino police pair in *Madigan*. Many of Don Siegel's movies have a quality of "facing" one another. In one film the lead will be a criminal psychopath (*Baby Face Nelson*) and in another he'll be an officer of the law (Widmark or Eastwood), or a whore will act like a nun (*Two Mules*) and a virgin will become a slut (*The Beguiled*).

Clint Eastwood's Harry Callahan is Siegel's *chef d'oeuvre*. Because he contains the characteristics of both hero and anti-hero and owing to the release of *Dirty Harry, The French Connection* and *Straw Dogs* within a relatively short period of time, Harry and the "heroes" of the other movies offended liberal sensibilities, at

Reni Santoni and Clint Eastwood hunt their quarry in DIRTY HARRY

the same time raising questions about how far a sense of personal justice should be allowed to go. Pauline Kael, reviewing in "The New Yorker," spoke out against unfettering the law: "Don Siegel is an accomplished exciter; once considered a liberal, he has now put his skills to work in a remarkably single-minded attack on liberal values, with each prejudicial detail in place."[5] The tone of the piece is set by the title "Saint Cop" and she describes Eastwood thus: "Six feet four of tough saint, blue-eyed and shaggy haired, with a rugged, creased, careworn face . . ."[6] Kael apparently feels betrayed by Siegel's (to her) switch from liberal to reactionary, and by Eastwood not remaining the identifiably malevolent killer of his Sergio Leone westerns.

Siegel makes two comments on *Harry*: " 'Dirty Harry' is a bigot. . . . He doesn't go in for all this fol-de-rol modern method of treating criminals. This doesn't mean that I agree with him."[7] And, "In the final analysis, what counts is the *number* of people that go to the film, like, say, in *Dirty Harry,* which is far and away the most successful picture I've ever made. I don't think the best. I like *The Beguiled* much better."[8]

Siegel's Charley Varrick, played by Walter Matthau, possesses all the virtues and sly vices of the anti-hero. Matthau is a charming, imaginative bank robber whose actions appear heroic in contrast to those of the Mafia henchman (Joe Don Baker). Matthau is also counsellor to Andy Robinson, depicted as a hot-headed, though less dangerous, version of his Scorpio killer from *Harry*. They are the criminal pair and fill the same functions as Eli Wallach and Robert Keith in *Line-up*.

Whatever qualities Harry incorporates, his is a view from the dark side of the mirror into which Charley Varrick looks. This fascination with evil and lawlessness is central to Siegel's filmmaking. The more corrupt and ruthless a character, the more attractive he is to the story teller in Siegel and thus, to his audiences.

Siegel has stated, "You see, most of my films aren't *about* any-thing,"[9] so that his movies evolve as complex plots, given depth by the rapid delineation of character for which he is noted and the viewer's concern for the outcome. *Invasion's* larger, sociological implications are anomalous to the Siegel *oeuvre*.

The two detectives in *Madigan* are as unscrupulous as the crim-inal because Siegel is more interested in what is secreted from view behind the "front" of the normal world. He knows that view-ers will enjoy his films more if the leads are less than honourable. Adroitly, he counters the unprincipled cops with the almost pro-fessorial (wire-rimmed glasses and tweed jacket), grocery-bag car-rying madman. It would have been easy for *The Line-up* to follow the heroin hunting routine of the two drab detectives, but it is more satisfying and intellectually stimulating to follow the insane Wallach and his advisor, who collects their victims' last words, to their doom.

For every proponent of irrational action in a Siegel film, there has been the obverse side of the coin up until 1971 when he made *The Beguiled* and unleashed the furies. In this, Clint Eastwood wasn't just a liar and an opportunist, trapped in a rotting Southern mansion by harpies. Although he became more manipulative reel by reel, he was outdone at every turn by the women of whom Sie-gel has said, "Women are capable of deceit, larceny, murder, any-thing. Behind that mask of innocence lurks just as much evil as you'll find in members of the Mafia. Any young girl, who looks perfectly harmless, is capable of murder."[10] As one sees the film the layers of duplicity, greed and sexual frustration are stripped away repeatedly until the film's core is revealed. There is unfor-tunately a corollary between the content of the film and its fate. The film didn't make any money, to Siegel's great chagrin. He wanted it released in art theatres and entered at festivals. It did well in France, but Universal didn't promote it properly in the

THE BEGUILED: Geraldine Page, Clint Eastwood, and Elizabeth Hartman

U.S.A. Siegel considers it his finest work to date, ". . . possibly the best I will ever do."[11] So frustration is the film's context internally and its effect externally, which is a great shame, as it is in a very different style for Siegel, certainly Gothic, but nevertheless revealing a facet which he'd not had a chance to exhibit before.

One stance is that everyone in differing degrees is compromised, tainted, dishonest; that we may be evaluated (by ourselves or others) by the success with which we hide our guilt from others and from ourselves, and that what we don't know about ourselves may

85

hurt us. In fact, this factor of "what we don't know about ourselves" is probably the most fascinating to Siegel. We have for examination a long line of quasi-heroes who are undermined by their own neuroses, psychoses and ignorance of themselves: Coogan, Madigan, Hogan (*Two Mules*), and McBurney who was beguiled.

In *Two Mules for Sister Sara*, the closest Siegel has come to comedy, Eastwood is almost playing his familiar good/bad man-with-no-name-or conscience. Also he fits the Siegel mould of being too unaware of his own motivation to protect himself and to maintain his code, "It's a great life. Women when I want 'em and none with the name of Hogan." His misogamy is thwarted by the disclosure that his beautiful travelling companion is a whore, not a nun, and thus available. In the end, he's captured, subdued, incapable of being the semi-lovable rogue he was at first. Prefixes like 'semi' and 'quasi' enter easily into any discussion of Siegel's films, since no person, no situation is black-and-white. The women in *The Beguiled* are not all bad; they are hard-pressed, unused to the lives they are leading, victimised by events they had no hand in shaping, sexually thwarted at the stages in their development when they should be freest. They can trust no friend, let alone foe: the Confederates who offer to guard them obviously have rape in mind and the Yankee in their midst acts like the master of a private seraglio. Why shouldn't they become desperate, say and do things they wouldn't under ordinary circumstances? *The Beguiled* is one example of neurosis run rampant. But whose neurosis? Where the ethical sands shift so quickly, who is the victim, who the predator? Ultimately, the subjects to which he is drawn, the manner in which they are filmed (*The Beguiled* is a study in tans and blues, the interiors suffused with muted sunlight), are informed and illuminated by Siegel's sensibility. It takes great courage to display one's innermost thoughts on film without flinching. Siegel will dare anything filmically; his movies transcend the impersonality of other, equally talented directors.

★ ★ ★

The view of life exemplified by these instances is the expression of a man who believes that the world is deranged, off-centre, spinning on an unaccustomed axis. Long before it was fashionable, Siegel presented insanity as a way of life, psychosis as a means of functioning and reacting in a world where sanity is not necessarily a valuable commodity. *Baby Face Nelson* has never been the kind of subject from which Hollywood would recoil, but the usual style was that of opprobrium or of explication as in *The Public Enemy* or *Little Caesar*. The *manner* in which Nelson's insane behaviour was presented makes the film one of the most honest portrayals of criminal lunacy ever achieved on film. Since then, of course, we have seen similar depictions of criminality in *The Line-up* and *Dirty Harry* (as well as in the films of Robert Aldrich, Sam Peckinpah, Samuel Fuller, Nicholas Ray) and in each case there has been no sociological apologia, no explanation by a criminologist or psychiatrist that "what you have just seen," etc.—was the product of slums or a misdirected youth. In fact the only "explanations" which the audience receives in Siegel's films come from (a) Robert Keith in *The Line-up* and (b) John Vernon as the Mayor in *Dirty Harry*. Vernon is what Lyndon Johnson called a "Nervous Nellie" and is a major source of aggravation to Harry as he insists on following the instructions in the Miranda-Escobedo laws to the letter.

Certainly if it is the *Hell* of war in which Steve McQueen chooses to live and allows himself to be blown up when the prospect of continuing in that microcosm is denied him, then the real world is in very bad shape. Another example of this derangement occurs in *Duel at Silver Creek*, which, though fast and punchy, is a weak film. Faith Domergue plays a siren who throttles a man to death after offering to nurse him lest he divulge information which would expose her accomplices.

An earth peopled by pods is the most terrifying, and logical, extension of the idea that society is dangerously askew. Evidence that we live in a world already inhabited largely by pods is thrust upon us daily, not only through films which can comfortably be labeled "science fiction," but through our fantasy machine, TV. Says Siegel: "The truth is that you are next. I don't care where you are, what country, sitting in the theatre or reading a movie magazine. There are pods and they are going to get you."[12] To another interviewer, he said, "So I'm becoming one of those people that I hate. I'm becoming a pod."[13] Siegel takes his fear of pods and of becoming one seriously. Speaking of *Madigan* he said, "I think anybody who's independent, regardless of their stature in life, is like that—who won't take it lying down, who talk back, fight back, who are not one of the large group of people who just go with the tide. You're much happier when you're not that kind of person—that's for certain."[14] *Invasion of the Body Snatchers* is recognised by leading critics and essayists as not only a classic of the *genre,* but as one of the best science-fiction films ever made.

In *The Killers,* Lee Marvin, Clu Gulager and the man who hired them (Ronald Reagan) illustrate the business world's view of what the work ethic, *in extremis,* promulgates. The two men cold-bloodedly knock off John Cassavetes and then, because Marvin's curiosity has been piqued by Cassavetes's failure to flee, they track down through unfolding layers of flashbacks, the story of respectability paid for with stolen cash, bartered sex and abandoned hopes. At each turn they are faced with corruption posing as honour. Like Robert Siodmak's 1946 version of Hemingway's story, the fatal woman is the dominant influence in undermining the integrity of all concerned. Siegel plays up this theme and uses Angie Dickinson, in the role of dual mistress to Cassavetes and Ron-

Siegel about to shoot a scene with Angie Dickinson and John Cassavetes in THE KILLERS

ald Reagan, as an icon of flashy sensuality, a rather obvious Eve.

Private Hell 36 operates on the criminal's premise that if you want something, take it. What Cochran wants is twofold: Ida Lupino and half of the $80,000 he stole from a cache of bills. The scene in which he and his partner (Howard Duff) find the money and then retrieve it from the gulley where it is blowing around wildly, is the most striking in the film. It is photographed by Burnett Guffey with a gritty detachment which enhances those qualities of irony and skepticism which Siegel brings to his best work. This shot is rather distantly echoed in *Baby Face Nelson* when

89

Mickey Rooney takes Sir Cedric Hardwicke out on the lake to drown him. In this scene the moon is low and makes long shimmering lines of light on the water as Rooney pushes the boat from the dock. Both scenes have a feeling of inevitability which Siegel's films possess as a general aura rather than as a stated fact.

This quality of detachment is one which has served Siegel well: "One of the things that possibly we learn as we get older is that it is, in a sense, a game. That, I think, saves me from the common complaint of fellow directors, which is ulcers. I don't have ulcers."[15] Neither has he the fame and honour which he deserves, though he is now receiving the critical acclaim he has long warranted. As he himself said in 1968, "I sometimes feel like a prophet without honour in my own land."[16] And to the audience at London's National Film Theatre: "I'd like you all to know that I'm deeply honoured. But where were you when I needed you?"[17]

Thus aloofness tinged with irony is a personality trait as well as an attitude to be found in Siegel's films. (Whether we get a worm's or bird's eye view of the action, these properties are very much in evidence.) They are sometimes ameliorated by what might pass for a more committed viewpoint on Siegel's part. His direction of the principal actors in *Madigan* is a case in point. In Henry Fonda's scenes with his mistress (Susan Clark), there is a feeling of struggling toward warmth, of trying to achieve emotional heights and falling short. In another context, James Whitmore berates Fonda, "What in the name of the living hell do you know about fatherhood?" Inger Stevens's furious outburst at Fonda, following her husband's (Richard Widmark) death, displays more warmth and interest in Widmark dead than when he was alive. As Fonda and Whitmore leave the hospital, Fonda remarks, "There's never any right thing to say, is there?" which is, at once, an expression of hopelessness and an acknowledgment that speech is inadequate to convey that which is deeply felt. However, those moments in his films in which Siegel's characters wrestle with their closely cherished beliefs or are forced to examine their motives and actions in a new light, are those wherein his gifts as a director are most evident. Although he rarely *tells* actors what to do, he elicits performances of great subtlety from them, even in roles which do not demand the degree of care he gives to them.

The deranged world, as in *Nelson,* is one where killers flourish, become heroes in the headlines and are as much admired as they are feared by a public ambivalent toward the glamour of crime. It is a milieu, as in *Private Hell 36* and *The Big Steal,* where cops are thieves and convicts can control a prison (*Riot*).

The gunman (Eli Wallach) of *Line-up,* carries a briefcase containing a revolver and silencer and discusses the use of the subjunctive with his mentor (Robert Keith). They look like businessmen, stay in motels and ride in rented cars, but both will die before their day's work is over, Keith by his crazed pupil's gun, Wallach bouncing down the side of an elevated highway. The framework of this film is one in which men in Chicago contract killers in Florida to collect heroin in San Francisco which has been smuggled in via the luggage of unsuspecting passengers from the Orient. *Madigan* shows the police threatening midgets, older women and kids with long hair; the Police Commissioner is involved in an adulterous affair, and his Chief of Detectives' son is on the take from a vice promoter. A minister's son is accused of molesting girls and an insane murderer uses a naked girl to distract two detectives, takes their guns and later shoots a patrolman.

A strong argument is made by the psychiatrist in *Invasion* that vegetable 'pods' should conquer the earth, reducing everyone to emotionless automatons incapable of those human qualities we believe to be prized by civilised mankind.

Clint Eastwood, as Coogan, is as ruthless as the criminals he stalks and in *The Beguiled* his life is circumscribed and ended by the women he believes he can control. These "ladies" may be more like men in every way than either men or women would like to acknowledge. They are sexually aggressive and are depicted as being able to run their lives, fend off intruders, farm their own land, educate themselves—to do themselves those things for which women have traditionally turned to men. These females have inverted their world; while they acknowledge the need for men, they are self-sufficient.

The idea of a whore who disguises herself as a nun—one who wants to dynamite trains, fight French soldiers and drink whiskey —as in *Two Mules*, is merely amusing and surprising. On the other hand, Eastwood's fanatical insistence on capturing the French gold, his adept handling of explosives and guns, his calm acceptance of the deaths he causes, are reasons for greater alarm.

A country in which snipers wearing peace symbols shoot innocents from rooftops (although we read of such incidents daily) is as dangerous, as disconcerting as any which Don Siegel has created. Dirty Harry is not one's favourite policeman; he's a loner contemptuous of the law he's supposed to uphold and ultimately rejects both it and his career.

Stranger on the Run depicts Henry Fonda as a drunken bum who is tossed off a train in a God-forsaken railroad town. He soon finds himself framed for murder and sent running into the desert as a sort of blood sport for the railroad sheriff's jaded thugs. He is helped by a Negro wagehand and later by a woman who doesn't want her son following in the sheriff's footsteps. This is a land where the blind show the way and good, supported by a power as weak as itself, can triumph.

Although made for television, *Stranger* shows that Siegel gave it as much attention as any of his best feature works. Its muted tans, dusty atmosphere and the feeling of most of the inhabitants that the town is in the grip of a force stronger than itself pervades the film. It is a movie which parallels much in Siegel's feature film work.

The "pair" in this case consists of Michael Parks and Dan Duryea as representatives of railroad law. They can be likened to Widmark and Guardino in *Madigan*. Duryea tries to exert the same restraining influence on Parks as Guardino does on Widmark and is both more and less successful. He is unable to keep Parks from setting Fonda free to trek across the desert pursued by the railroad hooligans, but in the end, when all the chips are down, he has a slightly dampening effect on the violence. Here again, is the moment within a Siegel film when a protagonist's rage can be made to work for or against him. With Widmark, the rage was usually counterproductive, but Parks is somewhat more tractable and there is no final shootout which would be the logical end to a film which had progressed along these lines.

Part of this change is due to the effect which Anne Baxter has had on the proceedings. Her son trails around admiringly in Parks's wake and she hopes that by giving him Fonda as a gentler, kinder, father substitute she can induce the son to give up his mistaken hero worship. But it is she who has to do all the work. She gives Fonda her husband's clothes and tries to put some spine into him by telling him not to feel so sorry for himself. Against her son's wishes, she helps Fonda in a gun battle, remaining cool and determined throughout.

The ending is a duel of close-ups between Parks and Fonda, as Duryea, Baxter and her son watch apprehensively. Enraged at losing control over the situation, Parks has struck Fonda to the ground, but a fight between the younger and older man is unthinkable (dramatically and from the director's standpoint). Because of Duryea's restraining example, Fonda's firm stance, and the sickening, unnecessary deaths, the son leaves with his mother as Fonda stands wavering in the centre of town. He runs to catch

up with her wagon and the final crane shot shows the three together while the train which might have carried Fonda off, still
a bum, puffs into the station. We can wonder at who is more of
a "man." Has the film turned in upon itself; has substance changed
or only appearance? Or does the close mark a regeneration for
Fonda through his newly adopted family? "I must be strong, for
they are stronger. I can no longer be a stranger on the run," sings
the title balladeer as the end credits appear, seeming to provide
an answer.

Parks and Duryea make an unlikely "police pair", not only because Parks is a borderline psychotic, but because of their physical and mental incongruities. Whereas Widmark and Guardino
(*Madigan*) were alike in age and in many aspects of their personalities, Parks is younger than Duryea, although the latter's superior. Duryea is also the counterpart of Robert Keith (*Line-up*) in
that he tries to counsel Parks, to soften his actions and to teach
him. In a sense, at the end, he has "taught" him, although Parks
may not be receptive to the lesson. Duryea is more directly related
to Lee J. Cobb's Lt. McElroy in *Coogan's Bluff,* always telling
Clint Eastwood to slow down, don't step on toes because he may
need help later. For every hyped-up man with a gun, be he criminal or cop, there is a temperate older figure who attempts to minimise the forseeable damage. I believe that Siegel's personality is
represented both by this calming influence and the active, sometimes destructive, force. Much admired by the actors he has worked
with, Siegel is the *bête noire* of many of his producers. He says,
"So I am my own producer . . . that's done in self defence . . . I
don't have to face the various idiots I'm forced to face."[18]

This remark refers to the statement in the opening section
about Siegel's rage at his own powerlessness in dealing with the
universe outside (and sometimes within) film-making. By constructing a narrow world in which good confronts evil, often with-

Siegel with Clint Eastwood

in the same personality, Siegel's films show the audience his preoccupations. The inward, personal conflicts of his troubled protagonists are resolved, or not, to the degree that Siegel is able to
believe in their ability to solve these problems. Where they are
insoluble, as in *Madigan* and *Hell Is for Heroes*, death is the outcome. The question of Coogan's relationship with the social worker is answered by concluding the narrative and Eastwood's leaving
without facing the issue directly.

★ ★ ★

I have put a great deal of emphasis on Don Siegel as the author
of his films. In view of the points raised it is impossible not to do

95

so. However, it would be unfair to minimise the contributions of his writers. Siegel works closely with them and values them highly. Speaking of Richard Collins and *Riot in Cell Block 11*, he says, "I moulded the script so that it would have the excitement it does have. I went out and wrote it at Folsom Prison and that gave it the sense of immediacy. There's a lot of me in the script and there's a great deal of Dick Collins. . . . there wasn't any question of who was writing what because he wrote it all, but I think he would admit that I contributed." Of *Invasion of the Body Snatchers*: "I worked very closely with Danny Mainwaring who's a very fine writer. Again we were helped and inspired by Walter Wanger. I'm very happy to talk about Walter Wanger . . . here I was working with a man who was educating me . . . Walter inspires one and he encourages creativity."[19]

★ ★ ★

Being collaborative, a film is the sum total of the efforts, and of the lives and experiences which shape it. In Siegel's films there are many recurring themes which cannot be ascribed to intelligences or sensibilities other than his own. Even *Annapolis Story*, "a disaster and a joke going in,"[20] has some of the energy and sureness associated with Siegel's direction. Siegel's best, most original films can be seen as efforts to come to grips with his own existential dilemmas. Recognising the circular, self-consuming nature of these absorptions, it is necessary to identify those areas in which he works most often. One area is that of relationships with women. One or two consistent female "types" appear in the best of his films. There may exist the whore or the virtuous woman, contained within the persona of one female or there may be two women, each embodying the contrasting personality types. *Private Hell 36* shows Ida Lupino, the self-confessed fortune hunter, contrasted with Dorothy Malone as the worried homebody. Even

ANNAPOLIS STORY: at right, Kevin McCarthy and John Derek

Siegel's first film, *The Verdict,* over which he had no control, depicts Joan Lorring, reminiscent of Mr. Hyde's "Champagne Ivy" (Miriam Hopkins in the 1931 *Jekyll and Hyde*), as flirtatious, grasping and thieving—she retrieves a gift she had given her boyfriend before his death and is caught in the act.

Initially Robert Mitchum is suspicious of Jane Greer in *The Big Steal* because of her early alliance with Patric Knowles, the villain of the piece. Mitchum learns he can trust her and the film takes off from there.

The sluttish Adele Mara of *Count the Hours* (1953) delineates unrefined avarice, coupled with ignorance, refusing to answer questions affecting the life and death of an innocent man until

Jack Elam in COUNT THE HOURS

promised a new dress. Teresa Wright throws her husband's gun into a lake because she thinks it may incriminate him in a murder and, although pregnant, she later dives repeatedly to reclaim it. Though Siegel had little control over this film (it was shot in only nine days) there is a consistency in the view that one from whom loyalty is expected could behave, even temporarily, contrary to a loved one's best interests.

In *The Gun Runners*, Eddie Albert's playmate and cover for his illegal activities (Gita Hall) is envious of Audie Murphy's secure relationship with his wife and self-knowingly covetous in her pursuit of the good life. Seen but briefly in *Hell Is for Heroes,* Michele Montan is likewise cunning and opportunistic. As a French barmaid, she is exposed as an intimate of the recently vanquished Germans by GI Steve McQueen.

Angie Dickinson is quintessential in her role of the shady lady who plays both ends toward the middle—herself. Appearing from nowhere, she eventually persuades a racer (John Cassavetes) to drive in a mail truck robbery. She uses her sensuality to convince Cassavetes to join the group, later betraying him and the rest so that she and master-mind Ronald Reagan can keep the proceeds. Siegel was unhappy with Dickinson's role: it "was not only dishonest, it was badly written. I was never able to make the part make sense. I couldn't resolve her part."[21] She relates to Cassavetes in many similar ways as other leading women to the men of *Private Hell 36, Beguiled, Two Mules, Hanged Man* and *Madigan,* inspiring their desire and at the same time their distrust and trying always to act in their own best interests. Frequently, and this is true of the men as well, their self-serving is turned against them, often just at the point of their success so that their triumph becomes meaningless (in Dickinson's case it leads to her death). Seen in this light, the role is worthwhile and typical of Siegel's cinematic feelings toward women.

No Time for Flowers (1952) is a largely unsuccessful attempt at comedy in which Viveca Lindfors portrays a Ninotchka-like Czech, eager for both advancement in the Communist world and for the luxuries of the West. In Jocelyn Brando, *China Venture* (1953) has the most straightforward female lead of all Don Siegel's films. Playing a nurse, she treks through hostile territory to find a Japanese officer whom she is required to operate on when the surgeon is wounded. There is a brief nod toward the possibility of a future romance with Edmond O'Brien; she asks to be thought of as a man, behaving simply and uncoquettishly.

Romantically equivocal, Dana Wynter lures and rebuffs Kevin McCarthy in *Invasion,* leading him to fall in love with her.

Viveca Lindfors (right) in NO TIME FOR FLOWERS

She is his faithful ally until the last reel when, after resisting the pods with all her strength, she succumbs and betrays him to the pursuing townspeople pods of Santa Mira. "I didn't know the real meaning of fear until I kissed Becky," McCarthy says of her and flees.

Vera Miles and Brenda Scott of *The Hanged Man* are nearly opposites: the former is wily, seductive, of uncertain ethics and motivation, prepared to use Robert Culp to undo her husband and to destroy them both in order to get money and the man she says she loves. Scott, a gypsy, reads Tarot cards and tries to beguile Culp with her omens. Away from these tokens, she's just another innocent girl with the potential for sex, and the ability to help— which she does, charmingly—or impede any man she meets. Says Siegel, "There are a lot of mystical, foolish young girls wandering around."[22]

The cause of Fonda's troubles in *Stranger on the Run* evolves from his quest for the town whore, whose brother he had met in jail. He brings a message to the girl, who is recuperating in a shack outside town from a beating administered by a man whose identity she perversely protects and whose name she dies without revealing. Ultimately he proves to be the meanest and ugliest of Parks' hooligans, Tom Reese. Reese wears an icongraphically confusing article of clothing—a white duster of the type still popular when the horseless carriage came on the scene.

Indirectly, through her mere existence and later through her mysterious death—after Fonda has indiscreetly asked for her whereabouts—this stock figure, the prostitute, minus a heart of gold, jeopardises an innocent man's life.

The whore appears later in *Death of a Gunfighter*, *Coogan's Bluff* and *Charley Varrick*. Like the white duster, she is a symbol of Siegel's attitude, not toward women, but to those women who exemplify the fragile social codes of that hypocritical public mo-

Inger Stevens vents her ire on Henry Fonda in MADIGAN

rality which is contradicted by their private deeds. The woman is employed by the railroad for the men's pleasure and usually resides in the hotel. Parks visits the prostitute to persuade her to reveal her attacker's name and to tell her how much "the boys miss you."

The same assailant is also, with Parks, an aspect of Fonda's potentially insane, grief-stricken other half. This composite persona is countered with the figure of the Negro (Bernie Hamilton) who is shot by the thug, while helping Fonda during a shootout. The white duster cancels out the black skin, who has briefly suggested the possibility of Fonda's regeneration in a speech about his "getting a second shot at" becoming a man again.

Inger Stevens, as Madigan's wife, although in love with and concerned for her husband, is shrewish and demanding, repeatedly creating a conflict between his feeling for her and his loyalty to the police force (and to the tough spot he is in *vis-à-vis* the killer who escaped with his gun). Sheree North, a still devoted ex-girl-friend of Widmark's, is more candid, asking him to stay at her apartment because he hasn't time to go home, even though he won't sleep with her. "I'm still in love with Julia." "Who's asking for love?" North comes back resignedly as he nods off.

"There was tremendous identification for me in the relationship between Widmark and Inger Stevens. Their marriage brought back vivid memories. I thought it was a very true one,"[23] says Siegel of working on *Madigan* and the near love/hate relationship of the couple. The implications of the plot designate theirs as the most destructive, least successful marriage in any Siegel film. Their love and need for each other cannot overcome the deep personality conflicts which drive them apart as they try to draw closer.

Clint Eastwood, as Coogan, flirts with a social worker, Susan Clark, because she's attractive and he's a sexual opportunist. On *Coogan's Bluff*, near the Cloisters, he gives her a clue to his enigmatic, closed-in personality, and in reward for his comparative openness, she kisses him. Later she resists his advances and when she's out of the room, he rifles her files for information leading to his quarry and leaves. Throughout the movie, Clark is sexually divided; aroused yet puritanical. She is strong, self-motivated, but stuck on an unyielding object (Eastwood) who is unable to return the kind of emotional alliance she seems ready to begin. When she shows up at 4 a.m. at his hotel door, angry because he's gotten Tisha Sterling in trouble with the probation board, Eastwood strikes to the core of her rage. He's recently been in Sterling's bed and it is Sterling's easy acceptance of her own sexuality which Clark is furious about. She wishes, Eastwood implies, that she had the same acceptance of her own sensuality which comes so naturally to Sterling.

At the end, waving goodbye to Eastwood's helicopter, we might wonder if she wishes she'd made love to him, or is she relieved not to confront this issue further?

Tisha Sterling, the girl-friend of Don Stroud (the fugitive), helps him escape Eastwood, squealing, "Kill him! Kill him!" Later Eastwood locates and seduces her, hoping to get information leading to Stroud. Sterling takes him to the pool hall where he's attacked by thugs; she watches the turmoil smiling noncommitally, as if in a private, drugged dream.

Siegel has used Marjorie Bennett twice as a stereotyped little old lady in tennis shoes. She arrives at the police station in *Coogan* to complain of rapists chasing her. When reminded that a detective had checked on her story, she yells, "He tried to rape me too!" As the widowed trailer park manager, she tells a disbelieving Charley Varrick, "There's mashers all over the place. They're after me all the time." The films and Siegel are commenting, through her, on the fears, fantasies and buried hopes, not only of oldsters, but of possibly a majority of women.

Shirley MacLaine, as the nun/prostitute of *Two Mules for Sister Sara*, travels in safety to the Juaristas she wants to help, protected by her disguise, but betraying her real vocation in several slips of the tongue and visual *non sequiturs*. We're not long in doubt that something is amiss; it is a question of time before Eastwood discovers her identity. The fact that he's surprised at all when she bursts through the door and announces, "This is no cat house. This is the best whore house in town!" is a verification of her masquerade's success and his credulity. After the battle in which his expertise vanquishes the hated French, Eastwood's sexual and emotional relief bring about his swift capitulation. In the last scene they ride off together—he with a dour expression on his face and his pack horse behind, MacLaine on the same mule but dressed in her tart's finery—red satin, black lace and with gaudy boxes as the pack horse's baggage. His and the film's last words are "Come on!" delivered in the same exasperated tone as when he first uttered them.

"You are a mule!" MacLaine sputtered when Eastwood refused to allow her time to find a fresh mule when hers went lame. In spite of her importance to his mission he won't acknowledge her brains and persistence, the fact that she's as quick with her mind as he is with his dynamite.

Don Siegel appears to polish off all of womankind for good in *The Beguiled*, crystalising his previous, divided opinions in this pictorialisation of the female's infinite capacity for deceit. Three of the women (Geraldine Page, Elizabeth Hartman and Jo Ann Harris) use Clint Eastwood for their own needs—sexual, emotional and physical. Page, the head of the crumbling Southern seminary where Union soldier Eastwood takes refuge, nourishes feelings of sexuality: "If this war goes on much longer, I'll forget what it's like to be a woman." But she tentatively offers him a job rebuilding the school at the war's end.

A repressed teacher (Hartman) although responsible for Eastwood's amputated leg, is the one he chooses. After making love in his barricaded bedroom, they announce their engagement at dinner. The *pièce de résistance* of this meal is the Yankee's favorite food, mushrooms, picked by the little girl (Pamelyn Ferdin) who discovered him while gathering some beyond the school's gates. We're left uncertain as to what caused Eastwood's death. Did Page and Ferdin fool the rest of the girls or were the mushrooms really poisonous? Page says softly, "I think probably his heart just gave out. He was in a very weakened condition." And Ferdin silences another question with an annoyed, "Do you think I can't tell bad mushrooms from good ones?" Too many rules were violated to

Siegel on location for CHARLEY VARRICK

permit Eastwood's survival or escape.

Just as there are no real heroes in Siegel's movies, there are fewer happy endings for these men. Even where the women are supportive, as in *Death of a Gunfighter* and *Baby Face Nelson*, the men are killed. Walter Matthau's wife is shot driving him away from the bank he has just robbed in *Charley Varrick*. The weak (and badly written) Audie Murphy character in *The Gun Runners* has a wife who defends and believes in him, but the context in which her character is conceived leaves her little room for another type of expression. Victoria Shaw of *Edge of Eternity* (1959) exists to provide romance and information for deputy sheriff Cornel Wilde who has to pursue her car to give her a speeding ticket.

This burst of high spirits is later seen as frivolous, for during this time a prospector was murdered near the spot where the chase began.

One might assume that these films are a way of clearing up a disturbed past or unhappy present. Siegel appears to have used some of his movies to describe his fantasy life, especially some unresolved feelings about women. Speaking of *Night unto Night,* Siegel says, "Then when I was directing the picture, I fell in love with Viveca [Lindfors]. Consequently, she could do no wrong and I was certainly not in any position to criticise her. I just sat back and enjoyed looking at her, and she was, I must say, particularly lovely. And I did very little directing."[24]

Throughout Siegel's most personal films runs a recurring strain: the protagonist is incapable of choosing the right woman. Repeatedly the hero confronts a woman with a strong will, personal problems, sexual hangups, conflicting desires; a female who either undercuts his capacity to function or who erodes his emotional stability. Seldom married, Siegel's men are free to meet women who are not what they seem to be, who are multifariously deceptive, misleading or destructive.

★ ★ ★

Don Siegel's films are also consistent in that, from film to film, there exists a deeply felt pessimism related to the futility of many of the protagonist's actions. These people are frequently seen at a dead end in their emotional or professional lives and see little hope of change or a meaningful future. They play out their dramas, sometimes in desperation, on the chance that what they do will improve their situations. Unlike the personae of a George Cukor or Anthony Mann movie, who are usually in transition, these characters are finite, locked into certain methods of behaviour and patterns of thought. They are fixed in Siegel's mind and not allowed any growth beyond his conception of them. Often, particularly in his more personal films, the individuals are completely separated from each other, performing their deeds in spiritual and sometimes physical isolation.

Frequently a time limit is placed, by himself or others, upon a protagonist's goal. He may need to keep himself, or opposing facets of his personality in some kind of balance until the feat is completed; or he may need to achieve something physically. Strong feelings of fate and doom pervade the atmosphere, deriving their forward thrust from the protagonist's need to perform certain inevitable actions. Often a character's original convictions, a cherished belief, will be turned against him at some crucial juncture in the plot, undermining either his future or his will to carry on.

When, pushed as far as he can go in his physical or emotional limits, a Siegel protagonist turns outside of his own resources for help, he is faced with two questions: "What is the real source of danger?" and "Where do I turn for help?" The answer to the first may be an external, physical threat or the risk of facing his own distorted personality, either through opposing an enemy who is out to get him or by trying to curb himself. The second question leads him to attempt confronting his internal problems at the same time that he's obliged to combat the threat from without.

Danger comes to Sidney Greenstreet in *The Verdict* in the form of George Coulouris who has supplanted the older man in his job. Greenstreet has reached the end of his career at Scotland Yard ignominiously, fired because evidence he gathered sent an innocent man to the gallows. Greenstreet tries to clear his own reputation and denigrate Coulouris by staging a murder the supercilious Coulouris won't be able to solve. The same tragedy—executing a blameless man—which caused Greenstreet to lose his position must not be repeated. Relief arrives through a friend (Peter Lorre) who realises Greenstreet is guilty and must be punished

Ronald Reagan and Viveca Lindfors in NIGHT UNTO NIGHT

although the victim was himself a murderer. The Siegel device of older and younger man is present, but the one (Coulouris) can't be taught humility except by a terrible example, and the other (Lorre) shows the more advanced Greenstreet the kindness and sad understanding needed to make him do the right thing. The dark, moody photography emphasises the characters' isolation and the London fog contributes to the ominous aura. To reinforce his solitude and the darker side of his personality, Greenstreet is sometimes viewed upwards, from under his paunch, or from the side.

Night unto Night is also heavily atmospheric, leaning on the

109

wind-whipped trees, pounding water and racing clouds of Florida before a hurricane for its threatening overtones. Viveca Lindfors and Ronald Reagan are alone by choice; she because she's haunted by the voice of her beloved dead husband, he because of his progressive epilepsy. Lindfors's state of mind prevents her from living fully in the present and from being able to return the affection Reagan needs. However, his love for her helps rid her of her husband's memory.

The perils of *The Big Steal* are real and external, albeit tongue in cheek, rather than psychological and internal. Robert Mitchum has to clear his name of a charge of absconding with $300,000 in military funds. He is chased by William Bendix, another hoodlum, supposedly in cahoots with Patric Knowles, who's really in possession of the money. Knowles's girl (Jane Greer), who distrusts him, teams up with Mitchum. They are in turn followed by Ramon Novarro and a younger cohort, playing suspicious Mexican police officers. Arriving at John Qualen's hideout where they are to split the money, Bendix shoots Knowles in the back, Mitchum and Bendix slug it out while Greer takes on Qualen, finally shooting him in the arm as Mitchum knocks out Bendix. Each event is hazardous; the real support for Mitchum, the man in the middle, comes from Greer who is as fast-talking, quick-thinking and light on her feet as any masculine lead. Jane Greer pitches in and gets her men, Qualen and Mitchum, who is cleared of the charges.

Big Brother's omnipresent eye is the chief threat of post-war Prague. His ally is the (by now) self-instilled fear of Communism and of saying anything which could be misconstrued. This provides Viveca Lindfors's would-be suitor with the title line. He's a restaurateur who brings her family gifts of food because "this is *no time for flowers*." Paul Christian is a more romantic lover, who is introduced to Lindfors by the party to tempt her with American luxuries away from the frugal life she leads. If she wavers she can't be trusted; if she's steadfast she'll turn him in. Through Christian's machinations, Lindfors and her family escape to the American zone.

The fear that one can incriminate oneself or others, no matter how innocent a remark may be, and that no one can be trusted, are the main causes for anxiety in this film. Coupled with economic deprivation, this spiritual poverty is even harder to bear. Existing with these tribulations is a good-hearted, more natural desire to be open, free to fall in love and to try for some happiness, however limited.

A variety of risks are depicted in *Duel at Silver Creek*. Susan Cabot is a tomboy who keeps an eye on the doings in her town and informs Audie Murphy and Sheriff Stephen McNally of possible trouble. McNally is endangered by his wounded gun arm and by Faith Domergue who tries to seduce him from his duties. Gerald Mohr, her putative brother, is extracting signed claims from neighbouring silver miners and then murdering them. Murphy helps McNally try to stop the slaughter until they argue. Later, Murphy wounds McNally while trying to save his life, and then kills one of the villains (Eugene Iglesias).

In this movie, solitude is equated with vulnerability in a straightforward manner. When Murphy, on an errand, leaves his father alone, the old man is shot by the bandits. Domergue strangles a wounded oldster when entrusted with nursing him. Alone with McNally, Domergue vamps him into forgetting his job, which gives her "brother" extra time for his sardonically performed looting. In a sense, McNally's gun hand abandons him by becoming lame after an injury, leaving him more open to assault.

Macdonald Carey is ostracised by his own townspeople when he takes on the case of an itinerant farm worker accused of murdering his employer in *Count the Hours*. The man is imperiled by his wife's loyalty and the people's desire to blame an outsider

111

for the murder of a fellow citizen. Carey's *fiancée* temporarily deserts him, but he continues working with the man's wife (Teresa Wright) to prove his client's innocence. Relief is provided through their persistence and through circumstance. One day before the execution, Carey's deadline, the exhausted Carey and Wright are talking in a saloon. A chance remark made by the bartender leads them to the evidence which clears the worker (John Craven). Adele Mara turns against her husband (Jack Elam) when Carey promises to buy her a dress for giving evidence to incriminate Elam in the murder.

Here the reiterated theme is of couples who are separated physically by circumstance, conviction or choice, as Wright and Craven, Carey and Dolores Moran, and Mara and Elam are respectively. Cinematographer John Alton outlines the solitariness of the figures against lake backgrounds, night skies, and highlighted interiors for dramatic emphasis.

Howard Thompson of "The New York Times" said, "Even with fairly thoughtful direction by Don Siegel, in addition to some nice raw photography throughout, this offering sacrifices substance of plain conviction for standardised suspense." Thompson blamed "the scenarists Doane H. Hoag and Karen DeWolf" for charting "the remaining action along familiar lines with the usual sideline nod to romance and an absurdly grotesque and obvious killer dragged to the fore in the nick of time."[25]

The Second World War as an arena for chance is effectively displayed when a soldier, left alone to man a radio, is killed by the Japanese who control the zone early in *China Venture*. The film fits few of the conventions listed however. A team of Marines and Navy men, led by Edmond O'Brien and Barry Sullivan and including Jocelyn Brando as a nurse, hasten through the jungle to reach a downed Japanese officer before his injuries can kill him. They travel through territory in which the villagers are too fright-

CHINA VENTURE: Edmond O'Brien and Jocelyn Brando

ened or hostile to give them information, even when bribed. *En route* the band is attacked by the Japs and, after locating the admiral (Philip Ahn) they are alternately befriended and menaced by a psychotic Chinese war lord (Leon Askin). On the way one man's arm is broken by a falling tree, there's a storm and the group loses its way in the heavy undergrowth. Siegel recalls that he went: ". . . all out on the hurricane scene. The studio was afraid the whole stage would float away."[26] And, regarding the jungle atmosphere: "All faked and I thought it was good. I have an eye for that . . . for composition . . . for how to get yourself wrapped around a tree without making it look as if it's a back-lot tree . . . staging a scene so that apparently you have great scope. I'm not

113

conscious that I'm doing anything remarkable. I'm just aware of the limitations of shooting . . . and I try to conceal them . . . If there's an area which looks weak, I decide I'll pan down to the feet of the guys walking and then, as I come up the area's good. At the moment where it's weak, I'm closest to the people."[27]

The surgeon is shot and during an operation on the Japanese admiral he has to relinquish his position to Brando. She completes the surgery under the doctor's direction while his arm bleeds through his dressing. Later, bargaining for time to let Ahn recover, and for more money to be flown in to appease Askin's greed, Sullivan and O'Brien have dinner in his tent. Looking at the officers for appreciative belches and signs of weakness, Askin drunkenly announces, "I like you. I like Americans. I like dollars. I do not like arguments." They try to outdrink him and then radio for more funds.

Except for an initial inter-service rivalry between Edmond O'Brien and Barry Sullivan which later gives way to mutual respect, there is a feeling of wartime camaraderie throughout the picture. They are willing to stop pulling rank for the good of the mission, and their ingenuity and Brando's perseverance are responsible for the group's success. O'Brien, taking the admiral and what remains of his party, leaves Sullivan behind as a hostage, to keep Askin inebriated and use the radio as a beacon for the pilot who will deliver the cash and hopefully rescue Sullivan. Askin discovers the trick and his men murder Sullivan. The band reaches the beach where the admiral is taken to a submarine. Ahn tells O'Brien that Japan is prepared to fight to the end, news which is relayed to Washington. The message is prophetic as the last shot is an exploding atomic bomb, ending the war and beginning the atomic age.

China Venture is an atypical Don Siegel film in several respects. Although there is an insane criminal type (Leon Askin) he has no opposite number among the American servicemen. O'Brien's and Sullivan's determination to do their job is not presented as an outgrowth of any abnormal personality trait. If Barry Sullivan's rank-pulling stiffness, overcome when the picture is two-thirds done, and his death at the hands of Askin and the Japanese (before which he shoots Askin in the back) are considered neurotic, then a hero has faced and killed his deranged other half. To me this is stretching the point, but it is not wholly unreasonable. Sullivan's and O'Brien's occasional flashes of temper are explained by the circumstances and negated by the growth of their respect for each other. The completion of the mission doesn't involve any change in conviction, nor is it thwarted, save that Sullivan is killed. The company is not doomed, simply threatened by the progression of events. Nor are the heroes—who are real, not anti-heroes—psychologically damaged. War may be the sphere which this group customarily inhabits, but as in more traditional Siegel films, the war is a deranged microcosm of a larger world. The only woman present is responsible for saving the admiral's life and is neither seductive nor fatal, rather the opposite, while retaining her femininity.

The special nature of wartime behaviour is shown by Edmond O'Brien when he shoots a wounded Japanese prisoner instead of allowing the doctor to administer morphine. Fate takes differing forms: the surrounding, powerful Japanese, the Chinese guerillas and their leader, the surgeon's wound, the storm and the deaths of the interpreter and the German shepherd trained to hunt Japs.

The riot in cell block 11 is caused by the explosive circumstances within a prison where men are given meaningless jobs or kept in forced idleness. Lack of money, no rehabilitation programmes, understaffing, and ill-trained, sometimes callous, guards are blamed for the situation. The cons have nothing to lose; life is intolerable and their demands are not unreasonable: better food

RIOT IN CELL BLOCK 11: Leo Gordon and Neville Brand

and recreational facilities, improved lighting, separation of the psychopaths (like the leader, Neville Brand's accomplice, Leo Gordon) from the ordinary prisoners and the renovation of the decrepit cell block where the riot originated.

Although acting as a mob, the prisoners are in reality loners who have a variety of motives for inciting the revolt. The most altruistic, (Neville Brand) wants better penitentiary conditions. So does the sincere, well-meaning warden (Emile Meyer) who is as much the victim of the episode as the convicts who riot. Leo Gordon, the psychotic half of the convict pair (with Brand), revolts for his own selfish reasons. Meyer, who has campaigned for

116

reform, is at odds with the state legislature and some of his own guards. As the insurrection spreads from block to block, time is running out for the rioters as the militia is called in. The governor, legislators and the warden try to reach a politically and ethically acceptable compromise, as a more aware convict populace attempts to make its voice heard. When the governor accedes to the prisoners' stipulations, the legislature repudiates the agreement. Brand, who had been told there would be no reprisals, faces a possible thirty years added to his sentence. Ultimately no solution to this dilemma is offered, as the convicts' hands are tied by the failure of the revolt.

Emile Meyer (like Brand and Gordon) can be seen as having an insane double in the person of Frank Faylen, the Senator who won't listen to Meyer or to the con's requests. One madman faces and menaces the other, when Gordon knifes Faylen in the arm.

Since both the outcome of *Riot* and the current state of American penology are well known (there have been some improvements, but seventeen years after the film was made, there was a revolt at New York's Attica prison), we see that there is no answer to the question "Where does help come from?" Not from the physically powerful, but psychologically and socially weak inmates. Nor from co-operative wardens, answerable to reformer governors who must accept the laws their legislatures pass. The public and state and federal legislatures are guilty of preferring to forget the squalour and waste, rather than confronting the issue and dealing with it openly.

Gordon Gow, commenting on "Individuals or Misfits?," the Fifties cycle of prison films, wrote: "Prison reform has been a continuing subject of importance in the U.S.A.; and indeed many other countries; and the Siegel film was memorable not only for its tremendous climactic action but also for the telling glints of individuals in the throng, faces marked with bitterness, carrying imputations greater than the immediate protest over food and cramped quarters, and implicitly questioned the value of punitive treatment as a cure for crime."[28]

The newspapers noted the film's realism and lack of unnecessary violence: ". . . although it need never take off its hat to any of its brash predecessors for lack of hard, cruel detail, it maintains so disciplined a grip on reality that it acquires the authority of a documentary. There is brutality—Brand's unhesitating action in stunning one prisoner who would prefer to remain neutral—yet brutality does not take over the picture. It is not there simply for its own sake but as a necessary and believable factor, as credible as a lead pipe."[29] And "Walter Wanger . . . armed himself with a forceful script by Richard Collins, a cast that appears to be perfectly at home in jail and Don Siegel, a director with the good sense to keep his players and story on the move, and transported this troupe to California's Folsom State Prison where most of the action was filmed."[30]

In *Private Hell 36,* Steve Cochran uses Ida Lupino's cupidity as an excuse and an impetus for taking $80,000 from a stolen cache he and his detective partner (Howard Duff) have recouped. He forces Duff to go along with him, hoping to use his half to finance a new life with Lupino. From this point on, his ruin is inevitable; a fact Lupino recognises as she tells him, near the close, "Maybe diamonds aren't that important." Her love for Cochran has over-ridden her initial passion for money, and she'd rather have him safe than risk his life to get her what she no longer wants. Until the denouement, she is unable to see beyond the strictures of her immediate cravings. Not only Lupino, but all the characters in the film are circumscribed and defined by their desires: Steve Cochran wants Lupino and the money to support her in style, and Howard Duff wants to be a good cop. The only people with ties are Duff, his wife Dorothy Malone and their daughter; Cochran is a bachelor on the prowl and Ida Lupino is a brassy nightclub singer. The latter two are shown living in furnished rooms; their connection with each other is one of their few links to the world outside of their jobs and their desires.

At the end, Cochran and the unwilling Duff are trapped at a trailer, the *Private Hell 36* of the title where Cochran has hidden the money, by their captain (Dean Jagger). Cochran is clearly the mad protagonist—pushed to the wall, like Madigan—meeting and being overcome by his saner double. There Cochran wounds Duff, who'd wanted to return the money, but is himself shot in the back by Jagger. This time the double is also the father figure, the Fonda/Whitmore combination, and Duff is the rational man between, the Guardino who survives in the later film.

Siegel, with Lupino and Collier Young who co-authored the script, demonstrates that love is not a refuge for man or woman, even for the couple (Duff and Dorothy Malone) whose marriage is threatened by Duff's anxiety and subsequent drinking. For Siegel, love apparently complicates more than it ameliorates the existential loneliness of his characters, creating for them additional hurdles in their already turbulent emotional lives and forming, rather than eroding, barriers to feeling and closeness.

Despite the upbeat framing story tacked on by the studio, *Invasion of the Body Snatchers* is almost unrelievedly doom-laden. (Says Siegel of this: "There was a great deal of laughter in the film. They took all that out."[31]) From the first encounter with the little boy, who's running from a woman he claims isn't his mother, to the track-out on the highway where Kevin McCarthy screams, "You're next!" to disbelieving motorists, the movie is a steady downward spiral of treachery and conniving by pods who have taken over the small California town of Santa Mira. (Mira means *look* in Spanish which is what the pods refuse to do and what McCarthy does to his peril. Examining anything—yourself, your life,

119

Kevin McCarthy and Dana Wynter in INVASION OF THE BODY SNATCHERS

your friends—is disastrous. The denial of the capacity for self-inspection is what makes a pod an inhuman, emotionless vegetable. "It exposed what a large group of people are doing to us culturally. They *are* pods. They have no soul and I'm sorry to say most people are that way. I think the pods outnumber us, if indeed we ourselves are not pods,"[32] Siegel has said.)

McCarthy renews a romance with high school sweetheart Dana Wynter, and together they are the last to hold out against becoming pods. They stay awake waiting for rescue by friends who, by their arrival, have turned into pods, and then flee through the hills away from Santa Mira. They're exhausted and Wynter falls asleep, waking in seconds as a pod. Voice over, McCarthy declares as he races away, "A moment's sleep and the girl I loved was an inhuman enemy bent on my destruction. That moment's sleep was death to Becky's soul, just as it had been for Jack and Teddy and Dan Kaufman and all the rest." Indeed even sleep, that cherished haven of rest and renewal is a deadly trap, for it is during sleep that one's mind is taken over by a pod duplicate. The fear of sleep is constant throughout the film; sleep is literally death, the destruction of one's spirit. Siegel on sleep: "We considered calling the film *Sleep No More*. The fear of sleep in the movie is the fear of waking up as a pod."[33]

All the shibboleths one is taught from childhood are turned inside out: relatives, friends and lovers are not benevolent; psychiatrists do not want to help their patients; sleep is not revivifying; your own house is not safe; your home town harbours enemy organisms which can rob you of your identity; plants are malevolent and have a life of their own; traffic cops and meter readers are in league with the enemy. Truly the whole world is conspiring to get you, to destroy your soul, your personality and your mind. Most of Siegel's films are negative and/or fatalistic, but *Invasion,* which grew not only from his own convictions, but from those of the producer Walter Wanger and the scriptwriter Daniel Mainwaring, is more explicitly so than any of his other films—except perhaps, *The Beguiled.*

As usual, the characters are insular, taking refuge not only in pod-ism, but self-protective by choice: McCarthy and Wynter recently returned from their respective divorces. McCarthy's nurse (Jean Willes), though married, is never seen with her family. Again, as in *Count the Hours,* the players are frequently photographed in isolation, standing in doorways, at railroad stations, bars, in cellars, on lawns, etc. The transformation into a lifeless pod merely exaggerates a previously existing condition. Santa Mira is at a dead end, the spread of the pods will exacerbate the town's decay, foretold at the opening by the littered vegetable stand, recently thriving, now abandoned. Through volition or inadvertence, becoming a vegetable means that one has become limited, not ongoing, and has curtailed risk and change as factors in one's life.

Although they jointly plan the murder of a common foe, the disturbed slum adolescents of *Crime in the Streets* (1956) are depicted as detached from each other. Their loveless, conflict-filled homes provide no respite from the tensions of the neighborhood. The closeness and poverty of the stifling apartments is a breeding ground for dissent. The film focuses on John Cassavetes, the most alienated of the teen-agers, as he masterminds the execution, huddling with Mark Rydell and Sal Mineo in dark alleys and on the fire escapes which provide temporary relief from the heat. Cassavetes's mother (Virginia Gregg) is more interested in her younger son (Peter Votrian) who admires and is rejected by his brother. Votrian makes some halting attempts to get close to his obviously troubled sibling, but is vigorously rebuffed. Mineo's sister (Denise Alexander) and a concerned social worker (James Whitmore) also try to make contact, feeling that some effort with the boy is necessary and worthwhile. Eventually, Whitmore breaks through and reaches Cassavetes in time to stop the killing.

The streets themselves are a "dead end," as they were for Humphrey Bogart and Sylvia Sidney nineteen years before in the film of the same name. Mean, dirty and claustrophobic, they offer no reprieve from overcrowding, nor any of the problems induced by poverty, neglect and lack of concern for others. Filmed entirely indoors, except the beginning, the sets augment the feel-

Opposite: John Cassavetes, Mark Rydell, and Sal Mineo in CRIME IN THE STREETS

ing of a neighbourhood without neighbours, of people who have long since stopped caring about life or themselves. Heredity and environment have irrevocably marked them as expendable—save for Whitmore, no one bothers. Cassavetes, obsessed with the idea that no one cares, is proved wrong. Whitmore and Votrian tangibly demonstrate their concern, and the final track out shows Whitmore and Cassavetes walking through the poorly lit streets together, presumably toward some kind of understanding and the possibility of psychiatric help for Cassavetes.

Mark Rydell, in a frenzy at the prospect of murder, is the insane extension of Cassavetes's personality, having the same relationship, though less importantly, as Leo Gordon does to Neville Brand in *Riot*. Mineo is worried, more cautious, but he does not have the temperate influence of the later mentor figures like Fess Parker in *Hell Is for Heroes*. As in *Heroes*, there is an implicit time limit: the point at which the protagonist will cross the boundary between sanity and madness. In both cases there is an inward struggle to fight up-surging anti-social instincts until some crisis point is past—in Cassavetes's case, he will cross the line when the "enemy" is murdered.

The leads in *Baby Face Nelson* are equally alienated from each other by suspicion and neurosis, and from society by virtue of their professions—robbery and murder. The only "pair" in this film are Mickey Rooney as Nelson and Carolyn Jones as his girl friend. She acts the Robert Keith half of the Keith/Wallach duo in *The Line-up*, trying to restrain her psychotic charge, playing a mothering or nurturing role, calming Rooney and attempting to prevent the execution of his wilder fancies. Her anxiety keeps him from shooting two boys who might be able to identify them.

Jack Elam and Sir Cedric Hardwicke are secluded by virtue of their equivocal status in their communities. Elam uses a blueprint company as both a respectable trade and as a front for providing floor plans, at a price, to the gang, also acting as their contact. He deals with Rooney and the rest by phone, and when his cover is blown, he collaborates with the FBI to frame his cohorts.

Mickey Rooney and Carolyn Jones in BABY FACE NELSON

Hardwicke is the seedy doctor who runs the sanatorium where Rooney recovers from injuries received in a hold up, and where his fingerprints are later removed. (An interesting case can be made for almost total loss of identity. Rooney wants to change his name, so he takes his girl's—Nelson. "Yeah! Why not? Anything's better than my old man's." She's always called him Baby and John Dillinger, then the leader, makes it Baby Face. Prints and name gone, eradication of self is nearly complete. Plastic surgery is suggested for his face, but rejected.) Hardwicke is at the bottom of his profession, consoling himself with alcohol and attempted passes at Carolyn Jones. Rooney threatens, "He'll be a patient here himself." His final isolation occurs when Rooney gets him drunk to steady his nerves and celebrate the success of the operation. In the lovely, lonely moonlight, Rooney rows him out onto a lake, and kills the old man to prevent his squealing later.

Even if they so desired, these people are incapable of altering their life styles, of modifying their aberrant personalities to conform to "normal" society. They end their days as they perpetuated them, on the wrong side of the law, fixed in the outmoded violence of the Thirties: conduct which was to become as anachronistic as the cars they drove. Nelson, Dillinger and their counterparts in the gangster films of the Thirties are the dinosaurs of the era. Their behaviour will soon give way to more fully organized crime, mechanised and dispassionate.

The protagonists' ruin is here inevitable. Even if we, the audience, weren't already aware of their fate, their actions would signal a bloody demise. Their inflexibility is as much responsible for this pre-destination as are the changing times. The advent of more sophisticated police practices and an aroused, irate populace showed the way to the end as clearly as their intransigent position outside society.

The "normal" world, on the other side of the terrain Siegel

usually works in, is depicted by him as not at all normal. As discussed earlier, the characters are counterpoised against an environment which is as deranged as they are. The straight world is as phoney, dishonest and evil as the criminal's, without the one quality which may be an improvement on the normal: they are honest about their lawlessness. They have come to terms with their lives, however crazily; they acknowledge their crookedness and have made some attempts to deal with it.

The Line-up embodies all the characteristics outlined previously. Eli Wallach's end is pre-determined by his psychopathology. Robert Keith says he's a "wonderful, pure psychological study. A killer with no inhibitions." And later, he's "an addict with a real big habit . . . H like in hate." It is this hatred which dooms Wallach, causing him to act rashly, to kill in the heat of anger and, finally, to turn on the father figure who has raised him, but who is unable to help him avoid disaster. Keith is limited by his association with Wallach, cast forever in the role of counselor/protector. His *raison d'être* is to supply the calming influence Wallach's hyped-up personality needs. Their symbiosis is a mutual neurosis; each gives what the other lacks. They are partially deficient. Wallach has neither scruples nor inhibitions; Keith is purely cerebral, having no physical abilities.

The force with which the qualities of impatience, insanity and the love of killing are projected on the screen gives the film its edge. Wallach is potent; the law, personified by stolid, greying Warner Anderson and Emile Meyer, is flabby. Except through superior manpower, the police are no match for Wallach's vigour and cruelty, or Keith's cunning and the help of their "wheel man" (Richard Jaeckel) (also dependent—on liquor—to steady his nerves) who transports them through San Francisco.

Typically, these three are revealed as solitary: Jaeckel drives alone in the front, Wallach confers with Keith on the handling of

127

Eli Wallach in THE LINE-UP

the next pick-up and then leaves Keith in the back seat of the car, striding off alone to his rendezvous, briefcase in hand. And they have a deadline. They must retrieve the heroin from the assorted carriers, make the drop at the aquarium and leave the city by 4:30 —the inspiration for Keith's recurring, calming line, "By 4:30 this will all be over." When they meet their end on the highway, a clock on the pier is just striking 4:30.

In *Edge of Eternity* the key elements of negativism and doom are played down. Partly because Victoria Shaw is cheerful and attractive, the aspect of onrushing fate seems less ominous. The murders near the mine shaft appear less fateful, especially with comic relief provided by Mickey Shaughnessy. There is a switch: the funny man is the killer, looking all the more baleful because we aren't used to this actor as a villain. Jack Elam, ordinarily the heavy, supplies information to Cornel Wilde, the hapless deputy sheriff trying to curtail a sudden string of deaths. At the close, as Wilde struggles with Shaughnessy in a miner's bucket dangling over the Grand Canyon, the sane man overcomes his mad other half and wins as Shaughnessy falls to his death.

Flaming Star is in the Siegel tradition: both Elvis Presley and Dolores Del Rio as his Kiowa mother are doomed because they fall between the conflicting worlds of the whites and the redskins. There is a great deal of poetry in the dialogue. The Indians speak of daylight as the time when "the sun has killed the stars" and both Del Rio and Presley want to die alone in the hills near their people, saying "I have seen the flaming star of death," indicating that they accept the fate, however unfair, that society has decreed for them. They are circumscribed by the whites' prejudice against their colour; John McIntire as the father and Steve Forrest as Presley's half-brother have more freedom because they are not Indians. Although the latter are asked to indicate which side they will choose in the coming war with the Indians, they are thought of as white. Presley and Del Rio don't have this option—in fact we never know how they think of themselves, being forced to see them as they are viewed either by the Kiowas or the white settlers. The implicit pessimism in this stance relates to the obvious bigotry of the whites (countered by the fair-mindedness of Rudolfo Acosta as the Indians' new leader), who insist on a kind of mindless podism—fight on our side (accept us) or we'll have to destroy you.

In *Hell Is for Heroes,* Don Siegel delineates the most futile of man's occupations and the kind of person who flourishes in this milieu. Steve McQueen is a psychopath, licensed to kill in the Second World War. In this situation he can unleash his natural anti-social instincts. McQueen can't exist as a normal human being outside the war and its opportunities for regimented murder, but he loses his life at the moment of his triumph.

McQueen is impelled by the need to have his belief vindicated; he thinks he can complete his single-handed assault on the German pill box which is keeping his squad pinned down. He has risked a field court martial and almost had a fist fight with his sane alter ego (Harry Guardino). When McQueen attempts the assault, both men (James Coburn and Mike Kellin) who crawl across and mark the mine field with him are killed. Coburn is

Nick Adams and Steve McQueen in HELL IS FOR HEROES

blown up by a mine—as McQueen reports to his superior (Fess Parker), Coburn was carrying a bazooka which ". . . lit up the whole countryside. Put us right on the block." Parker asks, "Were you right?" McQueen: "How the hell do I know?" Grimy, exhausted, almost in shock, McQueen slumps into his foxhole, clutching his rifle to his chest.

In the morning, with supporting fire and manpower, McQueen again charges the pillbox, hurling a satchel charge through the slit. The Germans toss the charge out. As McQueen runs back toward his side of the ridge, he's hit in the back and spins, flattening himself against a shell hole. McQueen staggers forward, eyes wide, mouth open, to throw the charge back through the opening. This time he succeeds, blowing the German soldiers and himself to a fugitive glory, or to the hell of the title.

The entire squad is depicted as finite; many of them die. While alive, the compatriots exist in separate foxholes, outlined against the night. There is some camaraderie, shown through the squad's makeshift efforts to fool the Germans into thinking there are more men across the demarcation line than actually exist. Bob Newhart does a phone monologue which is effective in this regard, but it is too long and vitiates the impact of the film.

The Gun Runners is not conventionally Siegel: Audie Murphy has a wife who loves him, and Everett Sloane, as his somewhat drink-sodden pal, provides companionship and help when the chips are down. Time is running out: Murphy's boat will be repossessed for non-payment of the mortgage, an eventuality which prompts him to enter into the gun-running scheme with crooked Eddie Albert, amusingly cast against type from his jovial second leads.

The Killers elaborates in detail ideas which were present in less developed form in Siegel's earlier movies. It is deeply pessimistic: everyone is compromised either through their associations, occupations or their pasts. Lee Marvin and Clu Gulager are the killers, hired by Ronald Reagan to murder John Cassavetes. When Marvin becomes curious at Cassavetes's refusal to flee, he and Gulager track down, through a series of flashbacks, the story of a mail robbery organised by Reagan. Cassavetes was wooed by Reagan's girl (Angie Dickinson) until he agreed to drive in the getaway, then was double-crossed out of his share of the loot. It is her duplicity which causes Cassavetes's disinterest in whether he lives or dies. When he is found by the killers, he's teaching in a school for the blind. The sightless students provide a clue to the film's symbolic stance: that none of the characters are able to "see" the situation they are in nor the fateful course ahead of them. And each is motivated by self-interest, so there is no possibility of co-operation between them. Cassavetes hasn't returned to his friend (Claude Akins) at the race track, preferring to end his life among the blind. Marvin and Gulager operate on hunches and clues, piecing events together until Marvin realizes there's enough money in the deal to retire on—he's ageing and will soon be too old to function as a hired assassin. Like any businessman, he wants to set aside a nest egg for his old age. Throughout the film, Gulager and Marvin look like normal businessmen, carrying briefcases, laundering their wash-and-wear shirts in hotel bathrooms, perfectly ordinary to all appearances but, underneath, brutal contract murderers.

Despite her earlier intimacy with Cassavetes, Dickinson knows that Reagan will be the survivor of the group. Although she prefers Cassavetes (the theme song running through their affair is "Too Little Time", and Marvin says repeatedly to those he encounters, "I haven't got the time," which is also a comment on the lives of the rest of the protagonists), she elects to stay with Reagan and help him with the double-cross, cutting out the other

Opposite: Lee Marvin in THE KILLERS

partners. Reagan and Dickinson, in separating themselves from their associates in crime, ensure that one day someone will want to catch up with them to collect the cash.

In each situation, the actions of one member of the group later go against them. Reagan and Dickinson are undone by the perseverance of Marvin and Gulager, Marvin is himself killed in the final shootout, Cassavetes is liquidated at the beginning. In every case, sticking together or relying on one another might have changed the outcome for each.

Similarly, Robert Culp in *The Hanged Man* and Henry Fonda, the *Stranger on the Run* of the title, are among the most solitary leads in any Siegel picture. Culp is trying to blackmail Edmond O'Brien (corpulent and vicious in this part, eleven years after his Marine Captain in *China Venture*) at Mardi Gras time. O'Brien's wife (Vera Miles) flirts with Culp and tries to persuade him to help her get enough money to escape O'Brien. Although she really wants to run away with Gene Raymond, she lets Culp believe she's interested in him. Culp is given a lift by J. Carroll Naish and Brenda Scott as a gypsy and his niece. He later shelters with them and has a wound dressed by them, so his loneliness is not total. Although surrounded by gaudy festival trappings, the film is essentially dark in feeling. Culp is on his unpalatable mission alone and is being tailed by an Internal Revenue agent (Norman Fell) who is also interested in the cheque, drawn on union funds, upon which Culp is basing his bribery scheme. The gypsies who aid Culp are depicted as basically helpless themselves. They have no money, are sleeping in a barn, and the girl is utterly unrealistic, laden with superstitions involving Tarot cards and omens. A note of irony is provided by Culp's choice of a hiding place for the cheque—inside a seldom-consulted reference book in a Christian Science Reading Room. This locale is visited by the lonely and friendless, and in fact seems to be doing fair business at Mardi

Gras, when people should be having fun.

In *Stranger*, Fonda is alone for the first half of the film, and then acquires Anne Baxter as an ally against the railroad thugs who would like to kill him because of what he knows. He is doomed by his self-imposed solitude, his self-pity and his dependence on liquor, but literally through "the love of a good woman," he is able to redeem himself and make some tentative steps toward rejoining civilised society.

Fonda is an exile, not only in the town, but in the world. He determined this condition at the time of his wife's death for which he feels unduly responsible. He has made himself impotent in dealing with life and is a fugitive from himself and from anyone who might threaten him by wanting closeness. When he saves Baxter's cow and calf during a difficult labour, his pride as a veterinarian is re-awakened. Baxter gives him her dead husband's clothes to make him more presentable and wearing them seems to inspirit him from within. She also recounts to Fonda a little of her family life with her son and husband before the latter's death, kindling in him the realisation of what he has denied himself. With his defeatism nearly vanquished, Fonda becomes "a new man," able to confront Michael Parks and able to decide, however belatedly, that joining a widow and boy on their farm is better than a life lived apart. He trades his dependence on alcohol for a commitment to living and the possibility of happiness.

Parks is also dependent—on his love of killing. His need to prove his leadership prompts him to send Fonda on horseback through the desert as sport for the hoodlums. Parks and his men are similarly isolated in the frontier town with little to occupy them but goading each other and harassing luckless intruders like Fonda.

With the exception of Fonda, who because of his original submissiveness was comparably rigid, these men are portrayed as static, not willing or able to modify their behaviour, enjoying their sadism and apathy. And it is fatal. Both Sal Mineo and Tom Reese die as a result of their devotion to Parks's authority, and Parks loses some of his control over the thugs because Fonda is able to regain his dignity and face him down in what would otherwise have been the climactic battle.

Duryea is more flexible. He is older, more temperate, less callous. He deplores what is happening to Parks and tries to mitigate the thug's behaviour by remonstrating with Parks. Through reminiscence and example, he attempts to point out that where he and Parks have been is better than where they are going. His is the voice of the philosophical, reflective man.

Madigan shows Siegel's customary adeptness with city locations. Richard Widmark and his partner (Harry Guardino) are working against a dual time limit. They have seventy-two hours to catch the killer (Steve Ihnat) who has escaped with their guns, and at the same time Widmark is fighting to subdue the maniacal side of his personality. Although Widmark is married, has a cohort and friends, he is portrayed as being essentially alone, working out his destiny and problems in isolation, struggling with internal furies as well as external physical trials. One of the most autobiographical of Siegel's putative heroes, he embodies the barely suppressed violence and actual sensitivity of a man destined to pick the wrong woman, fight the wrong fight against an enemy who has even fewer scruples than he (viz. the continuous war between Siegel and his producers, which he partially solved by becoming his own producer under a sympathetic aegis). It is this stand which destroys Widmark, and Siegel predicts the same end for himself. Referring to director William Wellman, he said: ". . . from what I do know of him he was a man who was severely hurt by his rebel attitude toward those in control . . . I think these people defeated him and I predict the same ultimate defeat for myself. People who have known Wellman . . . feel we are quite similar."[34] He seems to feel the oddness of his position as a rebel director in a large corporation and relates it, on screen, to those of his non-conformist hero/victims.

Siegel's view of each character in *Madigan* has a continuous blackness about it. Henry Fonda is a rigid man who has lived by the book throughout his career, in contrast to Richard Widmark who has always used his "policeman's discount." According to Fonda, "His clothes were always better than mine." Fonda takes an inflexible stand when the son of his lifelong friend and chief of

MADIGAN: showdown with a killer

detectives (James Whitmore) is compromised by a bribe. Fonda can't see the irony in the fact that his mistress is another man's wife. Siegel: "You know, he doesn't realise . . . Why shouldn't he be having an affair with this lovely girl? . . . he was to me very human, not stuffy."[35]

Fonda is secluded by choice; firstly in his somewhat exalted position, and secondly in his high-minded but ambiguous principles. He is a widower and the love of his young, attractive paramour is a new and exciting event in his conservative and personally unadventurous life.

Inger Stevens, instead of being Widmark's ally as his wife, undercuts him with complaints and nagging. She waits and worries alone in their apartment, evidently with little else to occupy her energies. Her frustration nearly leads her into adultery with Warren Stevens when Widmark leaves her in his care at a dance. As a couple, Widmark and Inger Stevens are consistent in their attitudes toward each other. Though both have opportunities for extra-marital sex, they reject them, preferring the uneasy and unsatisfactory kissing and fighting which comprises their marriage.

Widmark and Guardino first see Don Stroud seated alone in a movie. They threaten him into helping them locate Steve Ihnat, throwing him back on his resources and his instinct for survival to search the city for leads to Ihnat. Widmark tells him, "Right now you're a cop whether you like it or not." Stroud lives mostly on the wrong side of the law, procuring girls, helping Ihnat with a heist. It was the latter escapade which brought him to the attention of the midget (Michael Dunn) and thus to police scrutiny. Stroud is the link between Widmark and Ihnat, both dramatically and psychologically. Less crazy than Ihnat, and less criminal, he is also more deeply involved in crime, more demonstrably neurotic than Widmark. Stroud lives with his mother, but like Ihnat, "I move around a little bit too."

Fonda's mistress (Susan Clark) is more positive in the function she fills. While drawn sexually and emotionally to Fonda, she takes comfort in having a family. She relates most directly to Anne Baxter in *Stranger,* speaking softly with the voice of reason to Fonda's tirade against Whitmore's supposed betrayal: "What about you and me here in your bedroom? Is there a separate rule for us?"

Each character is compromised in some way. There is a moral or psychological defect, or the individual is undermined by his friends, or by his position *vis à vis* a given issue at a particular moment. All of these concurrent and shifting streams of emphasis make *Madigan* an unusually thoughtful film within a *genre* which has afforded Siegel, as well as other directors, a great deal of scope in the working out of detail (paradoxically it is a film he had little control over, although it exemplifies the themes which run through his most personal work).

In *Coogan's Bluff* Clint Eastwood is as devious and silent, as an Arizona deputy transplanted to New York, as Widmark is in his native territory. The fact that both are in New York City bears on their stories through the appearance of some colourful "types" whose aberrations are magnified under Siegel's scrutiny. While Widmark is able to use his knowledge of the city to his advantage, Eastwood is a fish out of water.

Typically Eastwood is a gallant misogamist, insensitive toward most people whose path he stomps across. These traits possess dangerous reverberations in that he comes closest to death following them to their implicit conclusions. Unused to the ways of the city, he is sapped in the Pan Am Building, losing his gun and his prisoner (like Madigan). He interferes with New York police practices; sticks up for a case worker (Susan Clark) who's being mishandled by Seymour Cassell at the precinct and, stumbling over James Edwards on some stairs, blows Edwards's cover as a wino staking out Betty Field's building. Each of these individuals is seen in isolation. Field is never with the fugitive son she so vehemently defends. Don Stroud makes and loses contact with his girlfriend (Tisha Sterling) three times in the film. Lee J. Cobb, as the police lieutenant whose boiling point gets lower each time he sees Eastwood, must deal with a variety of problems, not the least of which is seeing that Eastwood doesn't get killed breaking laws he has no regard for. They reach a point of grudging respect for each other after Eastwood has gotten his man the second time, but neither is sorry to see the last of his quasi-adversary.

Eastwood's assumption that he could stride into Manhattan, get his man and depart within hours, works to his disadvantage. By ignoring the local rules, he places himself in danger from unexpected sources. As unpleasant as he was in Arizona, his malefactors in the city are far less scrupulous, co-operative and beneficent. Eastwood gets a head wound, nearly loses his wallet to a hotel prostitute, and Field almost gets him with a flower pot. He is set upon by the thug buddies of escapee Stroud in a pool room, finally catching Stroud by swiping a motorcycle in Fort Tryon Park and chasing him through the autumn foliage and serpentine trails near the Cloisters. Like the cavalry, Cobb and the police arrive to cart Stroud off and finally Eastwood is able to leave this sinful city (to which he was introduced by a cabbie who tried to gyp him on the fare), having learned more than he will perhaps admit from the city slickers.

On Coogans' Bluff, overlooking the Cloisters, Eastwood tells the interested Clark of how he once saw "red, the colour of pity" oozing from his own flesh. He had let the wife of a prisoner he was travelling with say goodbye to her husband. She wielded a knife and Eastwood was wounded in an escape attempt. Since then, he implies, he's been especially wary. When Clark arrives at the Pan Am Heliport to say goodbye she is wearing red, and in his first display of "pity" Eastwood offers a cigarette to Stroud, handcuffed again to his wrist.

In this film Lee J. Cobb is the customary father figure, advising caution and functioning as Dan Duryea does in *Stranger*, correspondingly representing age, experience and even the same profession. Don Stroud is Eastwood's crazy other half, releasing his lunacy through his assault, escape and his dizzying motorcycle flight at the end. Stroud has two almost equally mad confreres (Tisha Sterling and David F. Doyle) who help him elude Eastwood. Sterling tries to have Eastwood mangled or killed when she takes him to the pool hall where Doyle leads the attack on him. Both relish mayhem, smiling appreciatively at the violence they cause.

In *Two Mules for Sister Sara*, Clint Eastwood is undermined by his willingness to believe the worst about most women and the best about a nun. "I sure wish I'd met up with you before you took to wearing them clothes and them vows." Despite occasional lapses, Shirley MacLaine maintains her pose as a bride of Jesus, increasing Eastwood's frustration. "I'm married to our Lord," she replies to his questions about her emotions and the possibility of sexual frustration. To this he responds, "I always knew women were liars, but I never knew about nuns till now." As she operates to remove a Yaqui arrow, he breathes, "You look like a beautiful woman, you smell like a woman" through a filter of whiskey anaesthesia. He loses control of himself and his emotions and is only too ready to surrender, given the opportunity.

Although Eastwood has no schedule on the day of July 6 when he rescues her from the bandits, MacLaine tells him that the soldiers at the fort in Chihuahua should be drunk on July 14, Bastille Day. He plans the Mexicans' seige that day. They join forces and later she learns of a French supply train which he hastens to blow up as it crosses a trestle, adding a second time limit to their journey. They are delayed by his wound, but reach the trestle in

*Mexicans vs. French garrison in TWO MULES FOR SISTER SARA.
Siegel behind camera operator*

time for MacLaine to climb up to place the dynamite on it. Because of the whiskey, Eastwood is too drunk to aim properly at the explosives and asks MacLaine to make him some coffee. Furious, the nun slugs the soldier of fortune, yelling "Sober up, you bastard!" and he fires, hitting the dynamite with his second shot.

Two Mules for Sister Sara doesn't share the fatalism and futility of many Siegel films. It's a comedy with a blacker side. Eastwood's surliness, his skill with and disposition to use dynamite, are contrasted with MacLaine's optimistic, rabid determination to have a part in the assault.

The film has more humour than many recent Siegel films. Siegel is an ironic, soft-spoken man with a known preference for the use of understatement and persuasion to get what he wants on and off the set. In Eastwood's manner he found the filmic mirror image of himself, and the mythic anti-hero of the soiled American dream to depict his Technicolor vision of the world we know but don't want to recognise.

All the male figures of *The Beguiled*, on or off screen, are treacherous, vanished or dead. Eastwood's death is linked visually to that of a male crow whose wing has been mending while it was tied to the railing of a widow's walk. The walk is one from which the girls, in shifts, watch for invaders, although the girl on duty failed to notice Pamelyn Ferdin as she helped the wounded Union soldier Eastwood to the gate. In flashbacks, which contradict his lies about his Quaker background, we see that Eastwood relished his Civil War opportunities to kill and burn.

Geraldine Page successfully thwarts the intrusion, in the guise of helping Southern gentlewomen, of a Confederate officer who, with his men, is evidently intent on rape or seduction. Page's brother, with whom she enjoyed an affair (shown in flashback), has apparently deserted. (Eastwood discovers the brother's love letters to his sister and taunts Page with them.) Elizabeth Hartman's father was a philanderer and Jo Ann Harris is the girl/slut who lures Eastwood to her bed. Hartman hears the sounds of their love-making and strikes him with a candelabrum as he limps past her from Harris's room. Eastwood crashes down the stairs, breaking his leg and necessitating the amputation which Page performs, with a certain perverse enjoyment, that night, by candlelight. Waking the next day to discover the horror of his missing leg, he screams "Why didn't you just kill me!" and vows sexual revenge on the household, declaring, "I'm going to be with any young lady who desires my company."

The Negro slave (Mae Mercer) bluntly rejects Eastwood: "The only way you'll have this black woman is dead!" Mercer has a dual purpose role: she acts as the surrogate father figure, giving advice to the girls while they're working in the garden. In the capacity of black female, hers is the only depiction of selfless love in the film. She recalls her lover with affection and warmth, the light in her eyes unlike the expressions of passion which we see in the others' faces.

Jo Ann Harris's aims are explicit. She intends to use Eastwood exactly as he wants to use her. Before he's even conscious during his first incarceration in the music room, she tells Mercer, who is sponging him to keep down his fever, "I might sponge some parts of him you wouldn't." When he's up and about, she makes a feeble excuse to leave her studies and corners him in an arbor, unbuttoning her blouse before she arrives, almost panting to offer herself to him.

Pamelyn Ferdin, who found the injured Eastwood propped among the trees where she was gathering mushrooms, is too young for sex, but at twelve she's "old enough for kisses," with which Eastwood silences her as a Confederate patrol passes their hiding place. Subsequently Ferdin tells Eastwood, "I've told Randolph all about you," causing wary dismay to cross his face. Randolph is her pet turtle and later in his anger at the amputation of his leg and his imprisonment, Eastwood smashes Randolph into the fireplace, turning her against him and inadvertently ensuring the cause of his own death. Eastwood's most sincere statement in the film, that he is truly sorry for the turtle's death, comes too late to save him.

Each deed the women perform is done with little consultation between them; often none. There is no extraneous dialogue, Siegel preferring to show rather than explain. Each figure in this microcosmic war is condemned to a perverse and specific solitude; Eastwood the lone male intruder who is desired by each of the women for different reasons. Page, Hartman and Harris have interests which are mostly physical, but extend to companionship and a desire for a strong labourer. Then there is Ferdin who is disillusioned after thinking she had found a friend; Mercer who has lost her lover to the war; Page's brother who apparently took his chances in fleeing incest and genteel poverty when he could. The male crow and turtle are the sole members of their sex present. The mushrooms take on a life of their own. They are the symbolic ashes from which Eastwood emerges and to which he is returned; possibly the instrument of his death and the place of his grave, whence he is carried by his survivors.

Eastwood's mad, self-destructive impulses are contained within himself, and some of these feelings are reflected in the females whom he tries to exploit. The women, particularly Page, are neurotic, not insane. They act out their emotions in revenge for Eastwood's attempt to take control. Time intrudes via the question: how long can Eastwood remain whole, devise a plan for survival even as he succumbs to his greed and lust? How long will the surrounding women allow him to flout their unspoken rules? Eastwood's assumption that he can act as he likes because they are alone and frustrated exists only in his mind. It is not shared by those into whose midst he was brought in a gesture of grudging kindness.

The mansion becomes a microcosm of the opposing sides of the war, which can be heard in the distance, but here the South is victorious. Eastwood's spatial limitations, combined with his physical disability and pride, are his undoing. Given more elbow room, he might have manoeuvered to a position of escape, psychic or actual. He could have realised that the women's mood had changed, that they were massing—consciously or not—to attack. The territorial imperative, in this light, is as important as Eastwood's incursion into the women's emotional terrain. Neither can be borne. Eastwood is the Northern enemy, a liar, an opportunist and sexually avaricious. The antagonists are thwarted at the time of the achievement of their implicit aims—to possess each other on their own terms—at the point when the other's subjugation is most imminent. In this, the most negative of Don Siegel's movies, the pessimism is infinite. No one is untainted; all are guilty.

Because of the difficulties it presents to liberal sensibilities, *Dirty Harry* should be defined partly in terms of its history and its effect on several reviewers. Many film critics, while acknowledging Siegel's evident directorial touches and the fine editing (with Carl Pingitore), were aghast at the film's explicit bigotry, blood-thirstiness and the steely savagery with which Clint Eastwood hunted Scorpio (based on San Francisco's Zodiac killer), played by Andy Robinson. These critics were equally appalled at the wishy-washy liberalism of the Mayor (John Vernon), who's at the mercy of recently enacted (Miranda and Escobedo) civil liberties legislation. Here are some quotes: "It is not so much the hard-hat sentiment that I find disturbing in all this so much as the dull-eyed insensitivity. *Dirty Harry* fails in simple credibility so often and on so many levels that it cannot even succeed (as I think it wants to succeed) as a study in perversely complementary psychoses." —Roger Greenspun, "The New York Times".[36] "It has such a sustained drive toward this righteous conclusion [that the maniac should be brutally eliminated] that it is an almost perfect piece of propaganda for para-legal police power . . . *Dirty Harry* is obviously just a *genre* movie, but this action *genre* has always had a fascist potential, and it has finally surfaced."—Pauline Kael, "The New

Andy Robinson receives a beating in DIRTY HARRY

Yorker".[37] "Is it too much to ask that these films [*Straw Dogs, The French Connection, Dirty Harry*] not be made? . . . we can all place some pressure on producers and distributors to stop offering us fascist propaganda and sado-masochistic wet dreams."—Garrett Epps, "The Harvard Crimson," reprinted with a rebuttal by Richard Leary in "Film Critic".[38]

Also noted were Siegel's careful and systematic use of San Francisco locations for Robinson's moments of seemingly random defiance of law and order. Greenspun commented on "Siegel's superb sense of the city, not as a place of moods, but as a theatre for action. There is a certain difficult integrity to his San Francisco, which is

not so beautiful to look at, but is fantastically intricate and intriguing—a challenging menace of towers and battlements and im-
probable walls . . . a desperate awareness that for this world the
only end of movement is in pain."[39]

The critics notwithstanding, *Dirty Harry* went on to become
1972's tenth largest money maker, racking up $6,392,199 in 750
playing weeks in the United States, according to "Variety." Not
all theatres across the U.S. were covered in this accounting and
the film actually made much more.

Of *Harry*, Siegel has this to say: "Well now, it's *extremely* unlikely that I'm going to do another one as successful." And: "But
we did it entirely off the lot, that is the Warner Bros. lot, and
when the picture was completed and was making a tremendous
amount of money, Warner Bros. came to me and said they didn't
think it right that I didn't own any of the picture and they gave
me a piece of the film, which is unheard of. I would say, on the
most conservative estimate, the percentage that I'll receive from
Warner Bros.—I'll have to net at least $200,000. So it's a tremen-
dous amount of money and I must say, it just floored me, because
I'm not used to being treated that way by majors."[40]

Although the philosophy is one which he repudiates, there are
elements about the movie—beside the money it has made—which
please Siegel. He says, "I have a theory that anybody can be a
killer. I decided I would do little touches which you may never
pick up: he wears a pair of black parachute boots with the white
lace going straight up in a military manner, very strange. I always
show him cleaning his boots, rubbing them on his pants leg. Maybe, this nut has come back from Vietnam, and what we see is a result of that experience. I may be criticised for—I got the largest
buckle I could get with a slightly lopsided peace symbol on it,
and I had my killer wear it . . . but it seems to me that it may re-
mind us that no matter how vicious a person is, when he looks

into the mirror, he's not capable of seeing the truth about himself . . . I always like my villains to be brighter than my heroes . . . he's quite brilliant, mysteriously so."[41]

Returning to the city from the country landscapes of his last two movies, which were made in Mexico and Louisiana, Siegel again used the rooftops, parks and alleys of San Francisco much as he had the highways, piers and residential streets of the same city thirteen years earlier in *The Line-up.* Siegel capitalised on the fact that Eastwood had no double, making us see that the ride six stories up the fireman's escalator to a would-be suicide is made by his star. In another scene Eastwood jumps from the bridge to the top of the moving bus full of kidnapped school-children. In *Harry* the director constantly mobilises both Eastwood's energy and the city's resources to excite and entertain the audience. The film is terse, full of colour and motion, at the same time utilising the viewer's willingness to be exploited emotionally by the casualness of the murderer's approach to his victims. Robinson/Scorpio doesn't care who he gets as long as the result is right for him—blackmail money and the thrill of eluding Eastwood/Harry, embodying the police force. *Dirty Harry* wrings its audience dry, as other films have tried and failed to do, by its manipulation of tension, pity and the desire to see "right" and "might" triumph over subterfuge and insanity.

Guardino and Vernon together represent the rational mentor, trying to curb the force of Eastwood's response to the killer's unbalanced criminality. As *Madigan* does, the anti-hero faces and conquers his mad counterpart, the difference being that Harry is a bigot with no respect for laws which protect a killer's right to be free if the methods used to apprehend him don't adhere to the letter of the law. It is, perhaps, as much his disgust at seeing what his crazy half is capable of as it is Eastwood's sane but bitter repugnance at the law-breaker which makes him react with such personal vengeance to the murderer's actions.

Although interpolated subtly in the dialogue of *Madigan*, the point is strongly made that Widmark is himself outside the law, in a relatively minor way. Widmark's indiscretions are moderate, open and paid back with a sort of humanity in which Harry never indulges unless he's mapping official points—the suicide rescue, the foiling of the bank robbery. Although Widmark extorts co-operation from a midget and the latter's secretary, he goes only as far as he must to get the desired result. Harry goes beyond that point to vanity and a sort of corruption of the spirit Madigan could never be guilty of. Witness Widmark's explanation of Harry Bellaver's phone call to offer help in the search for Steve Ihnat: "He was lonely." Widmark is capable of understanding and responding to needs other than his own. Eastwood's grim determination to do "what a man's gotta do" leads him to disgrace his badge, which is promptly tossed into the putrid water where Robinson is lying, and most importantly, allows him to be untrue to himself and his own best interests, professional and personal. Thus Widmark the humanist gives way to Eastwood the anti-human: the fury and savagery of blond, blue-eyed tarnished martyrdom to tall, blue-eyed, implacable determination. Some people have been opposed to the depiction of personal immorality which Eastwood represents, because it goes past our desire for safety from the terrors of everyday life to the release of what we all fear is the worst side of our own behaviour; *our* capacity to perpetrate our worst nightmares and our ultimate dehumanising of ourselves in the cause of some amorphous greater good. Harry is a fascist, Siegel is "an accomplished exciter"; but to what end? To entertain us and to point out that there's more than one way of seeing a cop. Harry is part of a long, evolutionary chain of movie detectives and his moral sense is no more spurious in its way than Sam Spade's, Philip Marlowe's or Captain Dan Tiger's (Murvyn Vye in Samuel Fuller's *Pickup on*

South Street). They have a job to do and they accomplish it with the means at hand.

Although the ingredients of pessimism, fate and the stricture of time are present in *Dirty Harry*, it's harder to take them as seriously as in Siegel's previous movies, because I think, Siegel himself doesn't take them as seriously. Harry is too cardboard for us to react to with the same dedication of purpose that Harry himself displays. We can't approach him on the level he would like us to, nor can we believe that Robinson is the menace the film thinks he is, despite evidence that mad gunmen like Robinson/ Scorpio are constantly with us. *Harry* is a less successful picture because it invites incredulity. The more personal *Riot in Cell Block 11* and *Madigan*, employing the same devices and using many of the same resources, receive respect because they ask less of our faith and, consequently, gain our admiration.

While Eastwood is on his self-appointed mission to protect San Francisco from Robinson, the antagonists face each other several times. In one encounter Eastwood stands, arms outstretched near a concrete cross, the parallel between the two figures being rather overdrawn. Eastwood argues with his superiors: John Larch as the Chief and John Vernon as the Mayor. He defies their orders not to use puritanical vengeance as a yardstick in hunting a criminal.

Robinson is always alone, tracking, sniping through his rifle's telescopic sight. We see him with one person, the black he hires to beat him in an attempt to frame Eastwood for police brutality. Siegel: "That was a macabre gesture . . . ironic that this psychopathic killer would go to a black and that the black would beat him without any feeling. He does a professional job. There is no anti-black feeling displayed by the killer. He calls the other man a black son of a bitch to try to excite him and get him to give him a worse beating."[42] Stalking their respective quarries or facing each other, the opponents are viewed as isolated from the life around

151

them. For a while, Eastwood has a partner (Reni Santoni) but, when Santoni is wounded and responds to his wife's request to leave the police, Eastwood is on his own again.

It appears that Siegel and Eastwood will have little reason to work together again. Having made four films with Siegel, Eastwood has since directed three, in the first of which, *Play Misty For Me*, Siegel has a small role as a bartender. (In *Charley Varrick* Siegel does a Hitchcockian walk-on as a sore loser at ping-pong.) He has made *Varrick* with Walter Matthau and filmed *The Black Windmill* with Michael Caine in England. In a sense Siegel and Eastwood and Eastwood have gone past each other, becoming stars of such magnitude in their respective crafts that they are too valuable for the studios to use on the same film for a fifth time. Eastwood has filmed a sequel to *Harry*, called *Magnum Force*, for Warners with another director (Ted Post).

Walter Matthau, as Charley Varrick, becomes a widower soon after the film begins. His wife (Jacqueline Scott) is shot by a policeman (whom she wounds after killing another) as she waits by a bank for Matthau and his young accomplice (Andy Robinson) to escape with the stolen money. She eludes the cops in a chase which goes through a fruit stand, sideswipes two cars and careens over rutted dirt roads before she dies. Arriving at their trailer site, Matthau leaves Robinson to prepare for their getaway. Matthau is readying his own solo exit from the area, evidently deciding that Robinson is unstable and a liability to a middle-aged pro.

The president (John Vernon) of the western bank chain which holds hot money until it can be "laundered," contacts a contractor for the Mafia (Joe Don Baker) to recoup the funds. Baker works and travels alone, picking up assignments in a variety of locales. Eventually Baker locates Robinson and beats him to death. Vernon is never seen with his superiors, but he does visit the manager of the looted branch (Woodrow Parfrey), the result of which is

Walter Matthau and Andy Robinson in CHARLEY VARRICK

that the manager feels pressured into committing suicide.

In his quest for papers to use in his flight, Matthau calls on an old man in a wheel chair (Tom Tully) who gives him the business card of a photographer (Sheree North) who also handles forgeries. Because he contemplates returning the money, Matthau contacts Vernon through his secretary (Felicia Farr). Although she dislikes Vernon, Farr has been having an affair with him. She's only too glad to accept the roses Matthau uses as a means of introduction and to sleep with him.

The film's most interesting female is the treacherous Sheree North, who milks Matthau of a large fee for the passports and

Walter Matthau carries out the robbery in disguise (left), and examines the haul (right) with Andy Robinson, in CHARLEY VARRICK

then turns him over to Baker in order to stay in the latter's good graces. Farr accepts and admires Matthau as the "last of the independents" (the film's subtitle and Matthau/Varrick's description of himself) and tells him not to trust her boss. Jacqueline Scott, "one hell of a driver," according to Robinson, relinquishes her life in her husband's arms. He softly kisses her goodbye before destroying her body and the escape car in an explosion designed to obliterate his and Robinson's trail.

Each character has chosen a life style which tends toward the maverick. Though they have daily contact with others, their professions and preferences keep them from real intimacy. Matthau and Scott, though long married, had been stunt pilots, then crop dusters—both solitary occupations—before taking to crime. Matthau lives in a mobile home and all his time after the robbery is devoted to clearing the way for his lone departure. All the relationships are tangential. People meet and part forever, usually after short associations and nine of them are dead at the film's close.

Children appear frequently in contexts peripheral to the plot of *Charley Varrick*. The credit sequence shows kids working early in the day, in a kind of normal prelude to the speed and violence of the robbery. Matthau's real life son races up to give the sheriff (William Schallert) the getaway car's licence number—which the boy had misread—and a small black boy whose dog has just died, watches Baker beat up his father in order to repossess the man's car. While waiting to see Parfrey, Vernon pushes a girl on a swing and Matthau buys the roses with which he woos Felicia Farr from a young sidewalk flower vendor. The children—innocent, helpful, polite—seem interpolated in the structure of the movie to point up the perversity of the deeds performed by the adults whose midst they are in.

These characters inhabit a hopelessly compromised world. Matthau is caught in a squeeze, typical of Siegel, between external forces—Robinson (who wants to keep the money) and the Mafia (which sends Baker to get it back). These outside organisations leave him isolated and dependent on his own ingenuity. In praising the picture, Vincent Canby of "The New York Times" said: "The fun in *Charley Varrick* is not sadistic, though there are cruel moments in it, but in watching Charley attempt to outwit both the cops and the Mafia. The casting of Matthau in this key role helps tremendously. Though Charley is tough enough to walk away from his wife's death without showing much emotion, the character is inhabited—maybe even transformed by Matthau's wit and sensitivity as an actor. If the role were played by someone else, *Charley Varrick* would be something else entirely."[43] John Vernon

155

is himself run down by Joe Don Baker who suspects him of being in collusion with Matthau. Robinson is undone by his own greed and Matthau's cunning in setting him up to take the heat.

Andy Robinson plays the apprentice to the older, wiser and cautious Matthau who also must face Baker, the aberrant man of action. This time, however, little emphasis is placed on this figure as being the alter ego of the anti-hero. Rather, Matthau is cool, rational, moving from one step to the next in his orderly progression toward freedom. On the contrary, Baker is an extension of both Vernon's and Robinson's personalities, being the cooler, controlling, sadistic version of what the youthful Robinson is in embryo form. And Baker is, too, the unleashed muscle of Vernon's seemingly calm Mafia ring leader. In this case, the killer murders both of his doppelgangers, but is himself outsmarted by the more temperate, resourceful Matthau.

★ ★ ★

The pervasive mood of many of Don Siegel's movies is that of alienation and loss. I think Siegel asks the question in his later films, "Loss of what?" and since he hasn't yet found a satisfactory answer, continues to make, not the same film repeatedly, but ones which explore the issues of loneliness, guilt, doom and man's quest for responses to problems which, because they are uniquely man-created, effectively have no solutions. The answer to the search lies in the continuing search itself, man's ability to carry on in the face of obstacles and to at last say, "I looked for an answer; I tried and I failed. I am unhappy, but I am satisfied because I made the effort."

It appears that, for Siegel, living in a physical and spiritual limbo, devoid of meaningful contact with one's fellow creatures, is a species of hell, a damnation. Nevertheless, this common human predicament is one to which he consigns almost all of his major characters and it is one which heightens the dramatic complications of his plots.

Isolation is unconquerable, immutable and it makes these individuals less flexible—backing them into psychological or actual corners. As undesirable as this condition may be, it is one Siegel's people rarely attempt to rid themselves of. Detachment gives them freedom of motion, a larger space in which to operate. It may restrict their options, but it also rids them of encumbering emotional ties. Madigan, Harry and Charley Varrick are essentially lone wolves who work best when nothing limits their independence.

The response to the issues of safety and danger is that perhaps nowhere can we find security; although maybe, if we are fortunate, we can find it within ourselves, since it is fruitless to seek it in others. Companionship and love have their place, but it is mistaken to see in these qualities either salvation or redemption and it is a disaster to expect either loyalty or sacrifice. If we are misled into a quest for respite from our dilemmas, we will be disappointed. If we look to others for the attributes we lack, or if we fail to find these traits within ourselves when we need them, the result is tragedy. The self-sufficient Harrys and Varricks know the answer and they are freed, even as they are tainted, by their lack of expectations. The absence of hope is the only hope.

All the protagonists, from Sidney Greenstreet and George Coulouris who are thwarted by their vanity in *The Verdict*, through the maniacal *Baby Face Nelson*, the withdrawn John Cassavetes of *Crime in the Streets*, to the later ferocious *Madigan* and *Dirty Harry*, and the calmer, but corrupted *Charley Varrick*, are the victims of their own vulnerability and, to a lesser degree, of circumstance.

They are caught in traps of their own making to which external tensions are applied. Although society at large is seldom implicated by defining the sphere in which the characters function, outside events influence the course of action. The individuals are weakened by their exposure to stresses beyond their control, as Ronald Reagan is impaired by epilepsy in *Night unto Night,* and as John Craven is menaced by hostile townsfolk in *Count the Hours. Madigan* is pressured into exceeding his already marginal caution by the police commissioner's deadline for catching the killer.

But ordinarily the *personae* of these films are fatally flawed from within. They are vain, arrogant, ignorant, dishonest, unmindful of what's taking place around them or they are almost mentally unbalanced. All the leading characters are undermined by traits inherent to their natures, and are thus prey to themselves, frustrating their labours and becoming, at last, inimical to their own interests.

★ ★ ★

In "Hollywood, The Haunted House," Paul Mayersberg prefaces his talk with Siegel by saying: "The director, Donald Siegel, who is I believe a highly talented man, is by Hollywood standards a failure, or at least unsuccessful . . . In talking about his career Don Siegel was preoccupied with his lack of success and the reasons for it: 'To give you an example, in consequence of having done special effects and second unit work I can never now [in 1967] as a director get anyone to do second unit for me. Producers always say, "Oh well, you know how to do all that. We don't need a second unit." So I have been forced to do a type of work that I don't like doing. I worked at Warner Brothers for fourteen and a half years and I still bear the scars.' "[44]

Mayersberg contrasts Siegel's career with that of John Sturges who directed *The Great Escape* and *Bad Day at Black Rock,* and then states: "Don Siegel has now virtually given up directing. He finds it impossible to get work. He has turned to television production with a series called 'The Legend of Jesse James.' You can see what the missing element is here, the element that might have given Don Siegel's story a happy ending. The best known guarantee for a happy end is a happy beginning and that's what's missing. For so many years Don Siegel didn't like what he was doing but he was unable (for whatever reasons) to do anything about it. Contrast this with the beginning of John Sturges who belongs to the same generation as Siegel. Why is it then, that Don Siegel (who is I believe a better director than John Sturges) can't really begin to do what he wants to? He himself feels that it's because he's a poor *entrepreneur*. He has the talent to make good pictures but not the other talent needed to get him to the point where he is able to make them."[45]

In 1968 Siegel told an interviewer: "As the world's worst entrepreneur, I've never been able to put together any project that's really mine. I have a Spanish story that I'm trying to get Belmondo for. It's a charming story but I don't think it'll ever see the light of day. I have a marvelous script that John Cassavetes wrote, which is a remake of *Crime without Passion* . . . but I can't get the studio to back it. They own it, by the way." Siegel goes on to praise, " . . . a new kind of spirit [at Universal]. I really feel that they want to do better things because they realise that they'll make a lot of money. And I think that's great."[46]

★ ★ ★

In an ironical and individual manner, Don Siegel has become an opponent of the Warner Bros. films he did montages and second units for in the late Thirties and early Forties. Then he usually worked on movies of social protest, historical or literary interest, and on films leading up to or about the Second World War. They often ended on an optimistic note, with the hero getting a job (*Blues in the Night*, 1941) or a French Humphrey Bogart completing a successful bombing mission (*Passage to Marseilles*, 1944). *The Roaring Twenties* (1939), however, contains one of

159

Siegel sets up the bathtub scene in COOGAN'S BLUFF, with Eastwood and Melodie Johnson

Siegel's darkest images: a giant tickertape crashes over Wall Street, bodies fall from buildings, announcing the crash of 1929 and parallelling the eventual ruin and demise of racketeer James Cagney.

Through their negative actions and impulses toward catastrophe, Siegel's protagonists, in moving toward their doom, are going away from the jubilant Cagney of *Yankee Doodle Dandy* (1942) and the unreflective cheerfulness of Ronald Reagan in *Knute Rockne, All American* (1940). As they draw back from optimism, self-sufficiency, the myth of success, they face the Humphrey Bogart of *Casablanca* (1943) who says, "I stick my neck out for no one." At the end of these characters' filmic odysseys, there is no heroic Paul Henreid to say, "Welcome back to the fight. This time I know our side will win." Granted that the three films cited were made in the shadow of the Second World War and by 1946, when Siegel made *The Verdict,* his first feature, the world was readying itself for the Marshall Plan and had a more jaundiced view of global realities. However, Siegel's pessimism pervades not only his films, but his statements to the press. About *Private Hell 36*: "I just felt a dissatisfaction with the picture. Probably my fault, really. But I wasn't happy on that picture; I was uneasy all the time."[47] Of *No Time for Flowers*: "This producer was more interested in making money as we were shooting the picture than in making money because the picture was a success. Apparently the money had been spent, but not on props for the picture."[48] Of the credit sequence for *Madigan*: "But, I had no control over it, none whatsoever, because by then, I wasn't talking to the producer."[49]

Siegel freely admits his anti-producer bias and since he produces his films, has a co-producer/production manager instead. The desire to control his movies, coupled with his intensified beliefs about the fallibility of human nature and the corruptibility of the spirit, have given Siegel a unique opportunity within the framework of the Hollywood studio film, to express himself with as much, sometimes more, freedom than any director of his generation.

★ ★ ★

Don Siegel has almost completed the circle he began with *The Verdict.* Matthau's casting as Varrick (Donald Sutherland was the first choice for the part) accomplished, through the differences in ages, something unforeseen, perhaps, but fortuitous. It had the same effect on the character's actions as the casting of Lee Marvin gave to *The Killers'* chief murderer, making Varrick's search for an escape route more desperate, at the same time more rational, than those of the younger accomplices who are killed in both films. For both men, breaking out of established modes is both a physical and existential process. The release sought by Marvin is almost attained through acting out the search, piecing together the jigsaw puzzle. For Matthau, the methods he uses to free himself from both his past and his present not only justify the end, but in effect begin to liberate him from the tainting memories of a past almost hermetic in its lack of implied sensuousness.

The London "Observer" critic, George Melly, writes of *Charley Varrick*: "Like an elderly tortoise he moves slowly and deliberately towards his goal. He leaves nothing to chance, but is only too aware that this in itself is no guarantee of success. He takes a low view of life, but has his feelings. . . . he has no qualms about destroying their corpses [Jacqueline Scott's and Andy Robinson's] to preserve his own living body."[50] However, we cannot assume that Matthau will fulfill any destiny beyond the confines of script and screen.

Audiences leaving a Siegel film are unable to say, "I bet Harry moved to another city" or "what happened to Harry Guardino after *Madigan* was killed?" Siegel's perception of these men, of the characters in his films, is finite. Just as there is no rationale behind *Baby Face Nelson*'s sadistic pleasure in killing, there is no reason why Clint Eastwood had to act the libertine in *The Beguiled*. He lived out his usefulness to the women, to Siegel and to the audience. Coming after *Coogan's Bluff*, *Harry* is an annihilation of the detective drama, made for the studio where Harry's predecessors grew up. Humphrey Bogart as Sam Spade (*The Maltese Falcon*, 1941) and Philip Marlowe (*The Big Sleep*, 1946) embraced the policeman's code even as he sneered at the detective's badge. Harry's rejection of both embodies his refusal to compromise his view of the ethics and duties of the police and his denial of a place for himself within that structure.

The fiery death of Widmark's Madigan is equivalent in meaning to the Siegel/Harry renunciation of Harry's shield. The protagonists in the movies between 1946 and 1971 are those whom

Siegel has used to develop and expose his black vision of human capacities. By making these movies, Siegel has been able to formulate a sort of relief for himself. The relative optimism of Matthau's escape from the Mafia killer in *Varrick* is a long way from the refutation of hope in *Harry*. *Dirty Harry* was perhaps the most fitting climax to the Siegel/Eastwood collaboration. Their complementary visions had both outlived and outstripped each other. Eastwood made *Play Misty For Me* (1971), a kind of small scale *Beguiled* in which the libidinous hero survives the onslaughts of a homicidally possessive female. *Varrick* represents a release of tension, not only from the fear of death, but from the emotional constraints of a dead-end present and a fond, though stale, marriage. The early work may be regarded as a carefully accumulated body of philosophical exposition. Siegel has taken the premises of the previous films and the reality of the world as he perceives it today for his later work. He has been freed to make those films which are closest to his evolving view of himself and to the place in filmmaking which he has designated as his, whatever that place may be.

Although he wrote to this author in November, 1972: "As one grows more successful there seems to be a desperate need to do better films. My feeling about *Charley Varrick* is it better be good,"[51] Paul Mayersberg was correct in 1967 when he wrote that Siegel had reached a dead-end, but that was before *Madigan* and it was the middle of the story. Neither *Charley Varrick* nor *The Black Windmill* are yet the end.

★ ★ ★

It is important to notice how Don Siegel photographs his heroes and anti-heroes as physical presences to point up his attitude. His relationship to other directors' viewpoints is helpful here. Howard Hawks usually shoots individuals from eye level rather than up to or down on them, maintaining a definite one to one relationship for the spectator. Siegel is fond of this approach also, but he varies it more often than Hawks. Fritz Lang favours eye level shots, but uses more close-ups, fewer two-shots than either of them. For me Don Siegel's work stands most directly beside that of Lang. They share a common pessimism in their view of humanity; in their belief that every relationship is tainted and that some kind of doom is inevitable no matter what one does to avoid it. The films of both men imply that being born is the first step toward corruption.

Since the two directors work in the action/western/crime genres, the parallels are easily drawn. Marlene Dietrich in *Rancho Notorious* (1952) is as ethical in the way she runs her criminals' retreat as Shirley MacLaine is playing the nun/whore in *Two Mules for Sister Sara*. Glenn Ford's fury at the death of his family in *The Big Heat* (1953), gives way to an obsessiveness which relates to that of Lee Marvin as he trails the stolen money in *The Killers*. In *Heat* Marvin portrays the thug who disfigures Gloria Grahame's face with hot coffee. He is almost equally psychotic in both roles, but his more advanced age and his search for a private pension plan makes him slightly less horrific in *The Killers*.

Whereas Hawks's lighting is seldom dramatic, Lang uses expressionistic effects to enhance the mood of a film. Siegel is in the middle, only employing high-key contrast when he wants to emphasise the importance of a particular moment. The most evident and one of the most effective is Ellsworth Fredericks's lighting of the greenhouse sequence in *Invasion of the Body Snatchers*. The greenhouse is dark and shadowy, yet illuminated so that every motion, every facial nuance is clearly defined. High contrast is used to emphasise the events taking place at that moment in the development of the characters. When McCarthy and Dana Wynter go downstairs from his office to the street, the spidery plants in the background are given heightened values and have an evil clarity. Kevin McCarthy makes his first *offensive* move against the pods when he stabs his double with a pitchfork. In another context this could be interpreted as a denial of identity, like Mickey Rooney's adopting a mixture of names to obliterate Lester Gillis in *Baby Face Nelson,* but McCarthy and Siegel make it clear that McCarthy is reaffirming his being, murdering the soulless replacement, and declaring war on the pods in Santa Mira. Most of the sequence is shot looking up at the characters as they advance down the row of plants, inspecting each individual seed-pod, now in the process of exploding out of their coverings and lying unfinished in a bed of protective foam. McCarthy's friends (King Donovan and Carolyn Jones) flee and McCarthy returns to the greenhouse to stab his pod, leaving the others' doubles behind. This advances the action, makes the violence less explicit, and serves to keep McCarthy from being labelled a murderer in any sense. More importantly, it is his first selfish act, the first time he has put himself ahead of others. The action erupts; McCarthy and Wynter flee to his car and we hear the police radio broadcast, see the cops leave the hamburger stand to take up the chase. We realise that there are few non-pods left in the town. The two spend the night awake in McCarthy's office and, during a police search, crouch in a closet, light coming through the grille down onto their faces, in effect, already in a jail of pod-like suspended animation. Their alienation from the townsfolk is reinforced in the morning. Farm trucks, converging on the central square, bear the newest crops of pods which are to be infiltrated into neighbouring communities by their relatives. This scene, silent except for the bull-horn voice of the cop who directs the distribution, is shot looking down past McCarthy's and Wynter's shoulders, as they speculate on their future and await the arrival of help.

Invasion tells us, turn around and the enemy you face is your girlfriend, your mother, yourself. You are doomed and the only reason to preserve your identity is to prove you haven't succumbed yet. Try, run, flee; you will be scorned and you will fail. The tacked-on ending mitigates nothing because the pods are all powerful and they succeed in their mission even as we make our last stand.

Siegel normally uses film graphics sparingly and unobtrusively. *Invasion* has a few notable crane shots: the arrival of McCarthy at the station accompanied by his voice-over narration which sets the stage for the ensuing events; and McCarthy's and Wynter's flight down the alley from the used car lot to the back stairs of his office. In both cases these isolate the characters from the action and the milieu around them. Returning home, McCarthy doesn't know what's happened and his nurse fills him in during the car ride from the station. The ride contains a low angle shot up at the car as the little boy (Bobby Clark) runs across the road in terrified flight from (what we later learn) is the knowledge that his mother is a pod. The shot stresses the relative sizes of car and child and the panic the boy feels. Another low angle takes in the littered vegetable stand which McCarthy's voice tells us had been thriving only months before. Both these shots and the information contained in their dialogue prepare us for the idea that McCarthy has come home to treat those of his patients who have not yet been transformed into pods. They don't appear for their appointments because by the time he gets back to Santa Mira the process has taken them over, too.

The second crane shot includes a slight horizontal pan following the running figures in the alley. They are limned in Fredericks's high-key lighting, their shadows growing longer as they near the stairs. The extended shadows increase the feeling of isolation which we feel in this scene; we know the pods are close behind, we feel McCarthy's and Wynter's terror, as though we are involved in the comforting conventions of traditional sci-fi films where the terror comes from "outer space" or from something anthropomorphic which we will soon recognise. Cinematographer Ellsworth Fredericks shot some scenes with such dramatically high-key lighting that they stand out in one's memory. The barbecue sequence is lit in a way that would be impossible in nature: light comes from various off-screen sources and even goes *up* through a trellis.

Ordinarily, when Siegel places a figure alone in a large space, he is both isolating the character and showing that character in motion. McCarthy walks across the train yard before we see a close-up of his face. We hear his voice before we know what he looks like (without the framing story opening°). Additionally, the credits descend against threatening clouds and Carmen Dragon's music is appropriately ominous, a quality it maintains throughout, pinpointing significant moments with an instrumental sting.

Siegel describes his preferred opening for *Madigan*: "I wanted to start it where the train came out at 96th Street, to have the titles over them going up the stairs and have the picture actually start when he kicks the door open."[52] Widmark and Guardino are isolated because they believe they are helping another precinct capture a criminal. They don't know Ihnat is wanted for murder until after they've lost their guns to him and been humiliated. The overt reason for their failure takes place so quickly it can almost be missed. Ihnat's in bed with a naked girl. To distract the detectives he sends her racing across the room. Eve swiftly triumphs over Adam; a pattern which is repeated with variations throughout the film. Siegel doesn't show Ihnat in spatial isolation again; he tells us that he's cooped up in various hotels around town, reitera-

---

° The film has been shown without the additional beginning and ending insisted upon by Allied Artists' producers Marvin and Walter Mirisch. These deletions were made at the discretion of the exhibitor and Siegel has expressed pleasure that it has been shown, at all, as it was intended.

167

ting the idea of aloneness verbally. Widmark and Guardino en-encounter other characters in differing states of solitude, notably the subway worker who gives them a lead and Michael Dunn and his bodyguard on a wintry boardwalk at Coney Island. Dunn is a midget and his response to Widmark's implied threat ("The longer he's [Ihnat] loose, the shorter your life span") is to agree, "Ahhh! I was gettin' sick of fresh air anyway." Siegel cast this part with a midget as a crook (in 1968 bookmaking was illegal), so Dunn is handicapped in at least four ways. He's a minor criminal who is crippled by his size, vulnerable to predators on both sides of the law (and Siegel makes it clear in this and ensuing scenes that the two sides are interchangeable), and isolated in Brooklyn. Even when he produces a lead—Don Stroud—to Ihnat, the conversation has all the overtones of threatening and pleading. Dunn's last words to Widmark are: "You make sure you give me a good funeral in case he makes me before you make him." Siegel shoots looking up at Widmark from Dunn's perspective to accentuate Widmark's intimidating position. The camera also shoots down on Dunn to stress his relaitonship to other people and objects of "normal" size.

The photography of *Two Mules for Sister Sara* not only emphasises distance spatially, but draws parallels between moral differences, physical traits, motor skills, intelligence and motivation in the service of stressing the real solitude of the two people travelling together and sleeping side by side in the deserts and mountains of Mexico. *Coogan's Bluff* creates this separation in the opening shots of Eastwood chasing the fugitive Indian across the Arizona desert, and then extends this hunt and his physical isolation to New York, where the roles of pursuer and pursued become blurred.

Siegel doesn't place his characters in a spatial or moral vacuum without letting us see why. There is always an accretion of detail and information, so that we know why we are provided with certain knowledge at a particular point. In *Coogan,* Don Stroud's mother (Betty Field) is seen in one room talking about her son. The black detective (James Edwards), posing as a drunken bum on the stairs of her building, is given no further identity than that of bum, then revealed as a detective when he screams to Lee J. Cobb that Eastwood ruined his cover by storming into the house to confront Field. The scene in Cobb's office, with Edwards still disguised, serves to further detach Eastwood from the mainstream of action in New York. He wasn't aware that he was flouting a rule when he acted rashly. Eastwood's abrupt appropriation of Manhattan, for the purpose of getting his man and leaving fast, serves to keep him there longer than he intends and longer than he might have if he'd done as he was told in the first place. He's still a stubborn "mule"; he doesn't listen. In effect, the longer he remains, the more isolated he becomes.

Comparably, there are no groups of any size or permanence in Siegel's films. As one is formed or shown (the French army in *Two Mules,* the small male clique in *The Verdict,* the Second Squad in *Hell Is for Heroes*), it is disbanded or destroyed. And these groups are physically alone. The French army is surrounded by hostile Mexicans and the Second Squad is abandoned on a ridge which Siegel depicts in a sweeping pan to delineate the extent of its insularity. Siegel shows us an entity in order to tell us that its demise is imminent. *Private Hell 36* introduces Howard Duff's family, but the next time they're together, we see that the guilt Duff feels is driving them apart. *Flaming Star* picks off the Burton family one by one to prove its thesis: that uncohesive groups atrophy or disappear. The surviving white settlers at the film's end are further proof. They are still threatened by the Indians and by their own code of racial superiority.

Unified groups fare no better. *The Line-up* shows a police department lineup which fails to elicit even one suspect and later,

Steve McQueen and Harry Guardino in HELL IS FOR HEROES

the disintegration of the team of killers. In death, Vaughn Taylor loses not only his life, he interrupts the continuity within his organisation. We see Taylor, a cripple in a wheelchair the same way we see Michael Dunn—with people nearby, but for a moment isolated in space, helpless because of a physical infirmity. These weaknesses are played upon by Siegel's use of, but lack of stress on, their social positions. As criminals, their disabilities reverberate against their anti-social status. Siegel is careful about the kinds of space he limits them to. Dunn isn't going to die, so he can be protected by his dumb blond guard, but Taylor will be killed, so he is seen furtively and slowly approaching the drop point in his chair.

170

The drop is an opening in a binnacle on display in Sutro's museum. Like Carolyn Jones apprehensively watching Mickey Rooney as he stalks the boys near their hideout in *Baby Face Nelson,* Wallach observes Taylor glide warily to the binnacle and stick his hand in, only to snatch it back when he finds nothing. Taylor resembles Wallach's accomplice (Robert Keith) and Keith's poking under the doll belonging to the little girl who inadvertently carried the heroin from the Orient, is visually allied with Taylor's probing the binnacle for something which, similarly, isn't there.

Siegel uses average-looking men as both hero and anti-hero. His only uncommon man, Clint Eastwood, is both the tallest and the one he worked the most with. The unlikely "heroes" of *The Verdict* were corpulent Sidney Greenstreet and tiny Peter Lorre, Warner Bros. hold-overs from their successful films with Humphrey Bogart. Notably, Mickey Rooney and Audie Murphy were short, but only in Rooney's case was this capitalised on. Kevin McCarthy and Robert Culp, like John Cassavetes, are the best "types" to exemplify a Siegel hero. Few of his male leads have been above average height: Mitchum, Eastwood, Howard Duff and Macdonald Carey.

Siegel doesn't glamourise his male leads. They look as though they live the kinds of existences the script says they live. *Madigan* inhabits a tacky apartment with Formica-topped furniture, and Patch (*Gunfighter*) seems to live in his jail. Howard Duff's home and his clothes look right for a Los Angeles detective with a family (*Private Hell 36*).

Don Siegel is scrupulous in not leading his audience to expect more from the characters than they will deliver. Logically, in all four Siegel/Eastwood films we never see Clint Eastwood in his home. He doesn't have one. When he arrives at a seedy hotel, it matches his expectations and ours. The hooker down the hall tries to lift his wallet and gets her arm twisted for her efforts. It does-

n't matter that *Coogan* is a fish out of water; he wouldn't be at home, or at ease anywhere. His expression of wariness and suspicion seems engraved on his face from a life spent looking over his shoulder to see who's sneaking up from behind.

The only females whom Siegel examines are in *The Beguiled* and they aren't "at home" either. They're in a seminary with the Civil War booming in the background. Geraldine Page who owns the school is worried about how to keep it going during the taxing period after the war. Why aren't the few remaining pupils with their families? No explanation, but it isn't important. We are meant to see these protagonists as having only the life Siegel allows them, not to wonder why they are isolated in a decaying mansion. Why do they continue their rituals of French lessons and table manners when these gifts will be useless later? Because what counts is doing, in being, and not necessarily in succeeding. Don Siegel himself knows what it feels like to believe you are not a success, to live in a kind of artistic limbo, knowing you are talented, wondering when recognition will come. Perhaps this is a partial explanation for the structure of his films; perhaps it explains very little about the man. "I mean it is very important that I do good work. I just am that kind of a guy. I have to aim for the moon. It doesn't mean that you're going to think it's good or that the audience at large is, but when that day happens, that audiences stop going to my films, then that's the day I'm through."[53]

Although nothing ameliorates his negative view of life, Don Siegel is a humanist, trying to work out his problems through his films, which in some way touch most of us. His is a vision of the world which is not unique. It is contemporary and relates to an acquisitive society. He treats women like men; they are as interested in control, money and sexual dominance as men are. This

Opposite: Siegel on location with Clint Eastwood for THE BEGUILED

seems to be Siegel's particular view, but it is a latent expression of "all men are brothers, but business is business" which is not unlike the Mafia code. This stance simplifies life, but it makes life less real; so that in the films events become more sharply defined and the performers more vivid than those in our own lives.

Siegel doesn't develop the "magic" in movie-making and prefers to show the strain that filming entails—not through clumsiness or by making a virtue of a vice. His films have a grittiness and tension that say, "This is all there is. This is what it's like." His movies' roughness enables us to see that there's a mind at work; that it isn't an effortless feat. The only "pretty" look is attained by some of Universal's mistier, softer preferences for achieving moods through the way film stock is printed.

Through the recurring themes discussed, Siegel seems to express his disappointment in life, but to say that it gives him freedom to make desperate, fatalistic films. "It takes a certain amount of courage to go to bat and face the hazards of making a picture. One of the most difficult jobs in the world is to do a good picture. I can't question my judgment. You just have to play it loose and be as well prepared as you can be and not lose confidence in yourself. And make the picture for yourself."[54]

Don Siegel's protagonists live on the raw edge of their nerves or by their wits, struggling to bring order to their chaotic existences or to control the warring sides of their personalities. There is always the danger of impulse gaining the upper hand, of an explosion at the point where a character asserts himself or is about to accomplish his goal. Where they are unable to achieve equilibrium, they fail, dying or becoming disgraced. Where these characters succeed, they are able to hold the opposing forces in check until some feat, perhaps of will, is completed. Through a catharsis of bullets to death, Siegel's male protagonists meet their fates, seeming to bear witness to Walt Kelly's Pogo who said, "We have met the enemy and it is us." The anti-heroes race to their doom the way Gary Cooper walked slowly toward his fate in *High Noon* (1952). This position makes Siegel a very modern director, as John Ford—whose fables of the West seem to have become tarnished—stylistically and through choice, was a less contemporary *auteur*. Siegel's films are smaller, tighter (whether Siegel or the budget dictated this) than those of Ford or Sam Peckinpah who with Howard Hawks and Fritz Lang have explored the same territory of violence and men among men and guns.

Ordinarily Siegel's heroes are somewhat taciturn, eschewing any rationale in dialogue or deeds for their behaviour. Where Ford's heroes are optimistic, courageous and loyal, Siegel's players are pessimistic, cautious and detached. Ford is sentimental, mythologising our past; Siegel is cynical, chipping away at the legends of success in urban America. Siegel's movies are not epic; they are small in scale, sometimes in budget and in the reputation of the stars who work with him. I intend no slur on the *ability* of his actors, only wishing to state that they weren't top attractions, except for Clint Eastwood, at the periods in their careers when they worked with Siegel. And clearly this is the way we recognise an *auteur;* the confidence that his name will carry the picture at the box office.

"It doesn't mean that I don't lose my temper and it [his qualities of irony and detachment] doesn't mean that I don't scream and it doesn't mean that I don't fight as hard as the next guy, but all the time I'm doing it, I know it's not the most important thing in the world. I can't question my judgment, and as I told you before, it's all a game anyway. So I'll get out there and do the best I can and the chips'll fall where they fall, I have to make it [the film] the way I think it should be made. I make pictures for myself. I don't make them for the front office. So that the result is, at least it's *my* film. It's the way I think it should be.

175

What the front office likes is a successful picture. They don't really care if it's good bad or indifferent. All I know is it's my best shot."[55]

★ ★ ★

The Black Windmill is without a doubt a continuation of themes in Don Siegel's previous films, but certain aspects of it suggest a less intransigent view point—a softening of attitudes. *Windmill* has more philosophical content than has existed in recent Siegel movies. The major issues are examined as alternatives to those raised heretofore. While remaining uniquely itself, *Windmill* has associations with Hitchcock's *The Man Who Knew Too Much* (the kidnapped child whose desperate parents go to great lengths to recover him) and *Foreign Correspondent* (quaint disused windmills and elderly government officials).

As the damaged and vulnerable protagonist, Michael Caine crosses and recrosses the line between hero and anti-hero. He is connected, not only with other Siegel heroes, but most pertinently with agent Harry Palmer in Sidney J. Furie's *The Ipcress File* (1965). In each picture, tape recordings play crucial roles as carriers of concealed clues, and in both Caine is exploited by older men whose plans for promotion have been thwarted, and who use him for material gain. In *Windmill*, Caine's activities are again hidden behind the facade of a respectable business. (This is the 'dirty underbelly' of society that suits Siegel's purposes here, a side which is, in reality, in constant danger of being exposed. Caine to his boss [Donald Pleasence]: "Do you think for one moment people don't know the name of your department and your title?")

It seems likely that Caine was cast precisely for his resonances in public memory with the earlier film. He acts the part like a Harry Palmer grown older; no longer on the loose, he's married, has a son, and is separated from his wife (Janet Suzman) *because*

Michael Caine and Delphine Seyrig in THE BLACK WINDMILL

of his job, that job of which he was so ironically despising nine years ago. Caine, as Major John Tarrant, this time plays it straight. His horn rims have given way to modish wire-rims and his waist is giving way to approaching middle-age.

Because he believes any emotional display will hurt his chances of locating his son (Paul Moss), Caine presents a muted facade as he moves through England and Paris, unleashing his rage and energy only on the kidnappers. Toward his nearly hysterical wife, he is reassuring and tender; to Pleasence he is cold

177

and correct; but with the abductors, he is merciless. At the instant of rescuing his boy, Caine embraces the ethical stances of both hero and anti-hero: threatening Joseph O'Conor's life, shooting John Vernon (the principal kidnapper) through a trap-door and blindly hitting his groin, then carrying his terrified child to safety. The price he pays for traversing these boundaries is that of rejoining the human race. If Caine is now more vulnerable, he is also infinitely more admirable; a profoundly shattered but more complete man.

Caine doesn't survive physically unscathed. During his meeting with John Vernon and his accomplice (Delphine Seyrig) in a Paris winery, he takes quite a beating. The briefcase carrying the diamonds (as ransom), which is rigged to explode at the release of a trigger, detonates when Vernon attacks Caine, bursting wine casks and knocking him unconscious. Caine is found with Seyrig's body in a hotel room, from whence he is taken to a hospital, badly banged up. Pleasence removes him from the hospital under arrest, gloating grimly over Caine's misfortune, to escort him back to England. From Pleasence's remarks, Caine realises he's the victim of an elaborate and, thus far, successful plot. Returning to London as a fugitive, he contacts Suzman, using a coded reference to Moss's making them see *The Sound of Music* several times. Although bitter—"I just hate what your job has done to you!"—Suzman volunteers to help; her feelings for her estranged husband have been reawakened. They become a single-minded team, physically separated but reunited in spirit.

Caine may be reborn, more capable of compassion, but we see *only* the happy ending, not its aftermath. Since it requires a major trauma to turn Caine into a feeling person, can the audience assume he is able to prolong this emotional state? Like all Siegel's films, *The Black Windmill* doesn't posit a future for its characters.

Opposite: Caine with Janet Suzman in THE BLACK WINDMILL

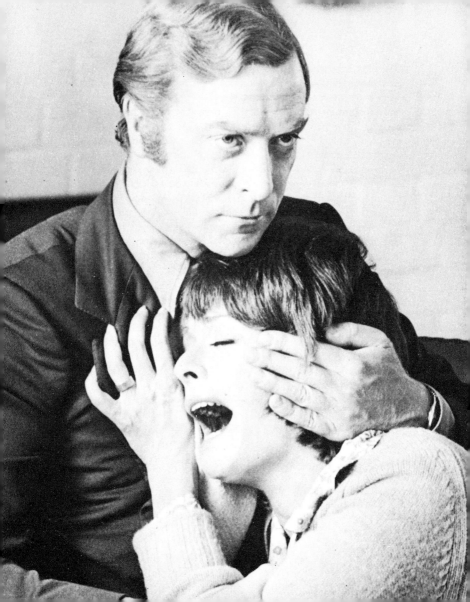

Windmill is as open-ended as *Dirty Harry* or *Charley Varrick*. As in these films and in their predecessors, Siegel adopts no moral viewpoint toward the protagonists, but there is an almost subliminal recognition on the audience's part that hero and villain have merged; their identities have fused. Is Caine a better person than Joseph O'Conor or John Vernon because he killed to save his son? Is Charley Varrick superior to Vernon or Joe Don Baker because he kills from expediency rather than pleasure or the profit motive? By remaining *outside* this issue, Siegel plants the inevitable suspicion that they are one and the same man.

As in *Varrick*, the hero's mad counterpart is split—this time into three people: Vernon, O'Conor and Pleasence. Varrick doesn't face his doubles until the end; Caine meets each at various points in the development of the narrative—Vernon first by telephone, later in Paris and finally at the windmill *dénouement* (Vernon himself is divided in three, employing Seyrig on both continents and one cohort in England, another in France). Caine encounters Pleasence frequently and with increasing hostility, although Pleasence, since he's coincidentally rather than purposely a villain, is not a direct victim of Caine's wrath, and is not present for the concluding shootout. As Vernon tells Pleasence during one of the crucial phone calls, "There's more than one Drabble."*

Joseph O'Conor, as the chief villain and insane architect of the entire scheme is partitioned into John Vernon, his sub-group, and Pleasence, an unwitting henchman. O'Conor and Caine meet first at a conference of the General Purposes Intelligence Committee, of which O'Conor is the Chairman and where Caine reports

* *Drabble* was the film's title until March, 1974, when the producers, Zanuck/Brown for Universal, reacting to preview cards and, perhaps, their own temerity, fed Universal's computer a lot of data and turned up *The Black Windmill* as the optimum title. Drabble was the combined identity of the kidnappers who phoned Caine and his wife.

on his get-together with Delphine Seyrig. They are reunited only once, when Caine traps him into the windmill rendezvous. There Caine faces and destroys his crazed doppelgangers. He shoots Vernon (O'Conor's death is inferred). Much less is made of the idea that Vernon and O'Conor represent Caine's insane other half unleashed than is the case in either *Madigan* or *Coogan's Bluff* where Richard Widmark and Clint Eastwood appeared relaxed in comparison to Caine's tightly wound manner as a repressed agent. Caine: "Isn't that what I was trained for? To hide my feelings?" Caine's real counterpart is the more inhibited Pleasence who sub-

THE BLACK WINDMILL: Caine with Donald Pleasence

limates himself in James Bond-like mechanisms (he shreds his used Kleenex) and a British passion for plants.

Herein lie the chief differences between *Windmill* and *Ipcress*. Palmer would have delivered the above line rudely, wielding the knife of sarcasm which is his main line of defence against his employers. Caine/Tarrant has to play his scene straight because his boy's life is at stake. Caine/Tarrant is Palmer with the wit cut out. He is also denied *Ipcress's* last scene which conveys a sense of ethical retribution, the balancing of accounts, and the film suffers as a result. A white knight in armour where the chinks are barely visible is not a really interesting figure, even though his actions leave one breathless. *Charley Varrick*, like all Siegel heroes, is morally tainted by his own existence and by the people that life forces him to deal with. Caine is in the ambiguous position of being both ethically superior and materially equal to—that is, guilty of criminal behaviour—those whom he revenges himself upon. Caine manages this feat with aplomb and earns our respect for the character at the same time. For raising and resolving issues of an equal moral complexity, Clint Eastwood's non-solution of the problem Susan Clark represents in *Coogan's Bluff* is a more realisitc conclusion for a Siegel hero to come to, particularly when there are no correlative changes on other levels to affirm Caine's regeneration.

Like *The Ipcress File*, *Windmill* is a film about *agents*, people who act in behalf of others and who become self-motivated only when their own interests are in jeopardy. The point at which a character becomes self-assertive is a critical one in Siegel's work. For Madigan it meant death; for Dirty Harry, defying the law he swore to uphold. To Caine, the step toward laying his ego on the line is taken only after more subtle methods have failed. Then he goes full blast—no longer Pleasence's hired hand, a soldier turned spy, Caine takes command of the action, a bit short-sightedly

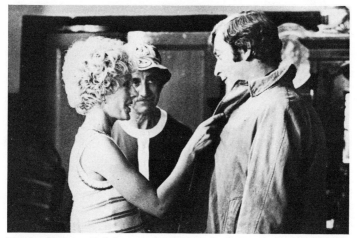

Siegel rehearsing Delphine Seyrig and Michael Caine on THE BLACK WINDMILL

as it develops.

Janet Suzman becomes Caine's surrogate to help him find their son. She takes the part with alacrity, receiving a coded phone call and pretending to visit a friend in order to slip away from the MI5 men watching her house. She rejoins her husband briefly for a bus ride during which they discuss strategy, parting so she can follow the clue Vernon let slip: "His room looks out on two rather unusual windmills." Suzman locates the site in an archive on historical monuments and phones Caine. He pauses just long enough to call Pleasence (and O'Conor), pretending to be Drabble. To Pleasence's protest that his is not the same voice as the previous caller's, Caine answers, "I told you before there was more than one Drabble!" O'Conor takes the bait and is surprised at dawn by Caine, wielding a tyre iron and threatening bloodshed. Agent meets agent; ageing egotism faces blind fury. Caine triumphs through surprise and energy, an energy which owes as much to his being younger as it does to being fuelled by rage. O'Conor: "Try to understand. I discovered they were going to axe me and put in a younger man. My capital's gone. My pension would hardly pay my wife's hairdresser. Don't you see?" Caine: "All I see is a deranged old fool who tortured my son!"

Like other Siegel films, danger comes from those close to the protagonist, rather than from exclusively outside forces. Caine is undermined, watched and apprehended by his employers and fellow agents. The sub-theme of agent vs. agent is deftly limned by Siegel during a brief chase into the Underground and out, when Caine, thinking he's eluded his MI5 pursuer, sees him in the next car. The MI5 gives an "I've got you!" wink of recognition, a wink which Caine returns when he ducks him later, slamming an iron gate in his face.

The components of dynamism and fate are at work here. They are embodied by Joseph O'Conor and his control over the events which shape the film. His is the Machiavellian hand which reaches out through Vernon and Seyrig, snatching the children at the aerodrome (Moss was with a schoolmate who is set free and ends up in hospital, babbling under the influence of LSD), torturing them, causing a car explosion on a highway, Seyrig's death, and Caine's pseudo-escape on the Bercy bridge over the Seine. Fate is people; their desires set in motion acts which change others' lives. Dynamism is conveyed through the energy expended by Caine and Vernon as they interact and try to out-guess each other.

Caine is related to Harry Callahan, whose chiefs make him relent in pursuing a criminal, and to Varrick, whose enemies are both close to him (his unseasoned partner) and separate (the Mafia group). Like Harry and Madigan, Caine is inimical to himself, relaxing his guard in the winery when he expects to find Paul Moss there and accidentally letting the armed briefcase detonate. He loses the jewels and the kidnappers, is injured and caught by Pleasence. Unlike Madigan, Caine's explosions of rage are productive, providing the impetus to go forward on his own, to get the diamonds, his son and his adversaries. Help derives only from his and Suzman's resourcefulness, their will to see Moss alive and safe.

Caine is alone, as are many Siegel heroes, increasingly cut off from the assistance of those he would normally turn to and thrown back on his own abilities and training. To emphasise this point, Caine is photographed in spatial isolation, striding through streets, in his apartment, in various types of transport and at the windmills.

The other principals are likewise solitary, especially Janet Suzman who waits at home for news of her endangered child. O'Conor is secluded at the top of his chain of command.

Less emphasis is placed here on the original assumptions of the protagonists being proved wrong than is usual in a Siegel movie. Pleasence believes Michael Caine is the brains behind the ransom plot, but a Scotland Yard man (Clive Revill) remarks, "Kidnapping his own son to extort money. That's too much for me." Joseph O'Conor thinks his scheme can succeed; Caine has little hope of a reconciliation between himself and Suzman; Seyrig is convinced that her sexual wiles can always prevail; Suzman thought that Caine's job meant more to him than either she or their son; and John Vernon is certain that he can survive and triumph, that no link in his chain is weak enough to break.

The picture's style is more subdued than in many of the other films. It is violent only in spurts, and the violence itself is less pronounced. Siegel's films are contemporary in the same way John Boorman's are, in that Siegel's affection for the mechanical artifacts of the twentieth century is echoed by Boorman's use of chrome as a reflective device and skyscrapers as temples of deceit and decay (*Point Blank*, 1967). Siegel lingers on the Hovercraft which brings Caine across the Channel. He uses the London travelator, the Underground, a police van and a barge laden with sand for Caine's escape.

The film is saturated with dark, rich colour, unlike the sometimes raw hues of *Varrick*, creating a mood which mirrors the characters' emotional involvement. There is more real romance between Caine and Suzman than Siegel has allowed in any previous film since *Death of a Gunfighter* (1969). This couple really care, not only for their son but for each other, and they show it on the screen.

Nevertheless, Siegel's rogue's gallery of women is complete. The most fatal woman, Catherine Schell as O'Conor's wife, is the least important, if one reckons by screen time. She is the cause of the machinations which comprise the plot, the Eve who lures her superannuated Adam to his doom, producing death and destruction through her (all-unknowing) existence.

Delphine Seyrig's every intention is malign: from her compromising smile directed at Michael Caine on their first encounter in her flat to the photograph of her naked on Caine's bed, planted by Vernon and then found in Caine's apartment by the Yard. There's a hint that her coolness masks a real indifference to men, no matter how she entices them through her provocative attitude.

Janet Suzman's lure is through love and the past she has shared with Caine. She is not fatal, nor does the film examine her in terms of her sexuality. Suzman is a warmer, more complete woman than any female since Susan Clark in *Madigan,* She is as fully realized a human being as any woman Siegel has ever depicted, but she shares a flaw common to all his women: she is other- rather than inner-directed. No Siegel woman lives for and of herself;

she is a satellite revolving around a male sun, her existence depends upon that man and when something happens to threaten the world of which he is the focus, she collapses, having no resources of her own to fall back on.

Suzman's part is brief, but her skill as an actress gives the role more dimension than is written into it. Perhaps the softening of intransigence which she represents indicates a willingness to compromise and grow, qualities which have heretofore been conspicuous by their absence in Don Siegel's movies.

Suzman proves strong, rising to the occasion and helps Caine locate their boy—when he needs her help. Caine's anguish is worse than if he didn't still love her, if he couldn't see Paul Moss's torment reflected in her, or if there were no child to provide a link between them. Suzman to Caine: "I know you love [him], maybe even more than I do."

The film's pessimism comes from elements that are familiar in Siegel's films: the use of ordinary surroundings in which to perform dark deeds; violence erupting in the sunlight, as in the kidnapping itself begun near a disused aerodrome, and the actions which follow—chases, theft, trysts—and the out-of-the-way London locales Siegel exploits to jog our consciousness (these could be *our* streets, *our* children, ourselves). Caine may be larger than life in some respects, but at bottom he's just another worried father. He's lucky that his job has fitted him for this particular business better than most men's.

What matters to the characters is survival on their own terms. They are a cold-blooded lot and their brutality is not exceptional in Siegel's cinema. They set about doing whatever is necessary to attain their goals, no matter what it entails. Their jobs and experience have trained for this usually violent flowering of their talents. Being unsympathetic means being invulnerable and implies the ability to endure. Similarly, letting down one's guard, even momentarily, foredooms one either to failure or death.

The story, based on holding and torturing a child for the sake of one man's continued life of ease and sexual pleasure, is a grim one. The use of claustrophobic settings helps to convey the sense of doom and lack of options for the protagonists: Pleasence's small office with its plants, document shredder and explosive briefcase on a shelf; the vintner's, ostensibly where Paul Moss is hidden, in reality a meeting place and nearly the site of Caine's ruin (he all but drowns in wine from the shattered casks); the black windmill itself, exposed on a lonely downs, hiding place for the kidnappers and maltreated boy, is intimidating in appearance, in the way it's photographed, and for what it portends. The conclusion partially ameliorates what has preceded it with father and son reunited and with hope for the future. Caine: "We're going back to Mother's. We both love you very much."

An audience watching a Don Siegel movie has the sense of coming in in the middle of an ongoing plot. The people seem to have always existed; they always will. The story continues even if we leave the theatre, though half the characters may be dead by the end. "We're going back to Mother's," says Michael Caine and we recall the last line in *Madigan* is Henry Fonda's to James Whitmore, "That's Monday."

O'Conor has reached an impasse in his job—he's being forcibly retired, an event which will be financially ruinous to him: "What does a man like me have to look forward to? My capital's gone."

Seyrig and Vernon literally reach blind alleys, expiring at the hands of their enemies; in Seyrig's case, at Vernon's option, when her usefulness is past. Vernon confronts Caine, his sane alter ego, and, failing in his mission to keep both the diamonds and the boy, is killed.

The deranged milieu inhabited by the protagonists is controlled and exemplified by Joseph O'Conor. It's his scheme, including Paul

Moss's torture over the phone, to support his prodigal life style and the wife he fears losing were that style to cease. To indulge his financial and sexual vanity, he co-opts Vernon and Seyrig, who steal, kill and kidnap for him, expecting not death but a share in the profits.

The Black Windmill is not an unqualified success. Coming after *Charley Varrick*'s purgative ferocity, one hopes for more than one gets. The number of substantive topics alluded to, but left unresolved at film's end, is too great to ignore. One wants to know as much about McKee, played by John Vernon, as one did about Boyle, the part played by the same actor in *Varrick*. And certainly we're entitled to some background on Janet Suzman, as Caine's long- but not nobly-suffering wife.

The film lacks humour, the saving grace of irony and perspective which Walter Matthau's Varrick had in abundance. The possibility of witty antagonism is raised by Caine's undeferential manner toward Pleasence, but carried no further.

Roy Budd's score, in particular a charming child's song, "Underneath the Spreading Chestnut Tree," is a vast improvement on Lalo Schifrin's drone for *Varrick*. Ousama Rawi's photography and Siegel's own selection of out-of-the-way locales are excellent.

More emphasis is placed on older men. Joseph O'Conor is related in spirit to Woodrow Parfrey, who tells John Vernon in *Charley Varrick*, "I can't start my life again." A number of the minor roles are cast with middle-aged men, and all the principals are forty or over, as *Madigan* used Fonda and Whitmore (even Widmark's lined face belied his agility and energy) and *Varrick* had Walter Matthau, Parfrey and Tom Tully. Siegel likes to use children, something he began in *Two Mules for Sister Sara* (there are singing children among the adults who carry the explosive *piñata* to the gate of the French garrison.) and has continued in varying degrees ever since. They were central to the plots of *The*

Beguiled and *Dirty Harry* (in the latter's bus kidnapping sequence), peripheral in *Varrick,* and though kept off the screen during most of *Windmill,* are of critical importance. The film begins and ends with Paul Moss.

At sixty-two, Don Siegel makes films that reflect himself, undiminished in vigour and in spirit. Although much of the philosophy his movies express is similar from film to film, he constantly invents new ways to communicate that pessimism which is inimitably his. But, says Siegel, "I'd like to do a love story, poignant, intimate. David Lean did *Brief Encounter* and *Ryan's Daughter,* both love stories. Mine would be more of a *Brief Encounter.* . . . I'm interested in small groups of people, not casts of thousands."[55]

Notes

[1] Stuart M Kaminsky, *Take One*, Canada, June 1972

[2] *Ibid.*

[3] Peter Bogdanovich, *Movie 15*, Great Britain, Spring 1968

[4] *Death of a Gunfighter* was directed by Robert Totten and Don Siegel. Siegel shot about one-half the footage in nine days after Totten and the star, Richard Widmark, had argued and Widmark refused to continue with Totten. Siegel wouldn't allow his name on the completd film and Universal invented a pseudonym.

[5] Pauline Kael, *The New Yorker,* January 15, 1972

[6] *Ibid.*

[7] Kaminsky, *op. cit.*

[8] Interview with the author, July 24 and July 31, 1972

[9] *Ibid.*

[10] Kaminsky, *op. cit.*

[11] *Ibid.*

[12] *Ibid.*

[13] Bogdanovich, *op. cit.*

[14] *Ibid.*

[15] Kass, *op. cit.*

[16] *Time*, November 15, 1968

[17] *Ibid.*

[18] Kass, *op. cit.*

[19] Bogdanovich, *op. cit.*

[20] Kass, *op. cit.*

[21] Bogdanovich, *op. cit.*

[22] Kaminsky, *op. cit.*

[23] Curtis Lee Hanson, *Cinema*, Spring 1968

24 Bogdanovich, *op. cit.*

25 *The New York Times,* June 24, 1953

26 Kaminsky, *op. cit.*

27 Bogdanovich, *op. cit.*

28 *Hollywood in the Fifties,* Tantivy Press/A. S. Barnes & Co., London/New York, 1971

29 Paul V. Beckley, *The New York Herald Tribune,* Feb. 19, 1954

30 A. H. Weiler, *The New York Times,* Feb. 19, 1954

31 Bogdanovich, *op. cit.*

32 Kass, *op. cit.*

33 Kaminsky, *op. cit.*

34 *Ibid.*

35 Bogdanovich, *op. cit.*

36 Roger Greenspun, Dec. 23, 1971, *The New York Times*

37 Kael, *op. cit.*

38 *Film Critic,* Vol. 1, No. 1, Sept.–Oct. 1972

39 Greenspun, *op. cit.*

40 Kass, *op. cit.*

41 Kaminsky, *op. cit.*

42 *Ibid.*

43 *The New York Times,* Oct. 20, 1973

44 Paul Mayersberg, *Hollywood, The Haunted House,* Stein and Day, New York, 1967

45 *Ibid.*

46 Bogdanovich, *op. cit.*

47 Hanson, *op. cit.*

48 Bogdanovich, *op. cit.*

49 *Ibid.*

50 *The Observer,* London, Sept. 23, 1973

51 Letter from Don Siegel to the author, November 2, 1972

52 Bogdanovich, *op. cit.*

53 Kass, *op. cit.*

54 *Ibid.*

55 *Ibid.*

56 Norman Taylor, "Suddenly, It's Siegel," *Film Review,* London, Dec. 1973

DON SIEGEL Filmography

STAR IN THE NIGHT (1945). A modern dress nativity converts skeptical motel owner to renewed faith. *Sc:* Saul Elkins (a story by Robert Finch). *With* J. Carroll Naish (*Nick Catapoli*), Donald Woods (*Stranger*), Anthony Caruso (*Jose Santos*), Richard Erdman (*Cowboy*). *Prod:* Gordon Hollingshead for Warner Bros. 20m.

HITLER LIVES? (1945). Montage–documentary of anti-German propaganda. *Narr:* Knox Manning. *Sc:* Saul Elkins. *Prod:* Vitaphone (Warner Bros). 20m.

THE VERDICT (1946). Detective who committed crime helps clear wrongly accused M.P. of murder. *Sc:* Peter Milne ("The Big Bow Mystery", a novel by Israel Zangwill). *Ph:* Ernest Haller. *Ed:* Thomas Reilly. *Mus:* Frederick Hollander. *With* Sidney Greenstreet (*George E. Grodman*), Peter Lorre (*Victor Emmric*), Joan Lorring (*Lottie*), George Coulouris (*Supt. Buckley*), Rosalind Ivan (*Mrs. Benson*), Paul Cavanaugh (*Clive Russell*), Arthur Shields (*Rev. Holbrook*), Morton Lowry (*Arthur Kendall*), Holmes

191

NIGHT UNTO NIGHT: Art Baker, Broderick Crawford, and Ronald Reagan

Herbert (*Sir William Dawson*), Art Foster (*P. C. Warren*), Clyde Cook (*Barney Cole*), Janet Murdoch (*Sister Brown*). *Prod:* William Jacobs for Warner Bros. 86m.

NIGHT UNTO NIGHT (1949). Woman haunted by dead husband leases her Florida home to epileptic scientist, leading to romance. *Sc:* Kathryn Scola (from a novel by Philip Wylie). *Ph:* Peverell Marley. *Art dir:* Hugh Reticker. *Ed:* Thomas Reilly. *Mus:* Franz Waxman. *With* Ronald Reagan (*John Galen*), Viveca Lindfors (*Ann Gracy*), Broderick Crawford (*Shawn*), Rosemary DeCamp (*Thalia*), Osa Massen (*Lisa*), Art Baker (*Dr. Poole*), Craig Stevens (*Tony*), Erskine Sanford (*Dr. Altheim*), Ann Burr (*Willa*), Johnny McGovern (*Willie*), 192

Lillian Yarbo (*Josephine*), Ross Ford (*Bellboy*), Irving Bacon (*Real Estate Agent*), Almira Sessions (*Maid*), Dick Elliott (*Motel Manager*), Lois Austin (*Mrs. Rose*). *Prod:* Owen Crump for Warner Bros. 92m.

THE BIG STEAL (1949). Quadruple chase after stolen loot across Mexico. *Sc:* Geoffrey Homes [Daniel Mainwaring] and Gerald Drayson Adams ("Saturday Evening Post" story, "The Road to Carmichaels" by Richard Wormster). *Ph:* Harry J. Wild. *Art dirs:* Albert S. D'Agostino, Ralph Berger. *Ed:* Samuel E. Beetley. *With* Robert Mitchum (*Lt. Duke Halliday*), Jane Greer (*Joan Graham*), William Bendix (*Capt. Vincent Blake*). Patric Knowles (*Jim Fiske*), Ramon Novarro (*Colonel Ortega*), Don Alvarado (*Ruiz*), John Qualen (*Julius Seton*), Pasqual Garcia Pena (*Manuel*). *Prod:* Jack J. Gross for RKO. 71m.

NO TIME FOR FLOWERS (1952). Prague-based romantic comedy of anti-Communist intrigue. *Sc:* Laszlo Vadnay, Hans Wilhelm. *Ph:* Toni Braun. *Art dir:* Eduard Stolba. *Eds:* Arthur Nadel, Henrietta Brunsch. *Mus:* Herschel Burke Gilbert. *With* Viveca Lindfors (*Anna Svoboda*), Paul Christian (*Karl Marek*), Ludwig Stossel (*Papa Svoboda*), Adrienne Gessner (*Mama Svoboda*), Peter Preses (*Emil Dadak*), Manfred Inger (*Kudelka*), Peter Czeyke (*Stefan Svoboda*), Frederick Berger (*Anton Novotny*), Oscar Wegrostek (*Johann Burian*), Helmet Janatsch (*Milo*), Karl Bachmann (*Lawyer*), Hilda Jaeger (*Mrs. Pilski*), Pepi Clockner-Kramer (*Flower Woman*), Reinhold Siegert (*Police Guard*), Willi Schumann (*Police Sergeant*), Ilka Windisch (*Woman Drunk*), Toni Mitterwurzer (*Sedlacek*), Theodore Prokop (*Czech Peasant*), Robert Eckertt (*Taxi Driver*), Peter Brand (*1st Soldier*), Karl Schwetter (*2nd Soldier*). *Prod:* Mort Briskin for RKO. 83m.

DUEL AT SILVER CREEK (1952). Sheriff and gunslinger foil silver mine claim jumpers. *Sc:* Gerald Drayson Adams, Joseph Hoffman (from a story by Gerald Drayson Adams). *Ph:* Irving Glassberg. *Art dirs:* Bernard Herzbrun and Alexander Golitzen. *Ed:* Russell Schoengarth. *Mus:* Hans J. Salter. *With* Audie Murphy (*Silver Kid*), Faith Domergue (*Opal Lacy*), Stephen McNally (*Lightning Tyrone*), Susan Cabot (*Dusty Fargo*), Gerald Mohr (*Rod Lacy*), Eugene Iglesias (*Johnny Sombrero*), Walter Sande (*Peter Fargo*), Lee Marvin (*Tinhorn Burgess*). *Prod:* Leonard Goldstein for Universal. 77m. Technicolor.

COUNT THE HOURS (GB: EVERY MINUTE COUNTS) (1953). Ranch hand cleared of murdering boss by pregnant wife and lawyer. *Sc:* Doane R. Hoag, Karen de Wolf (from a story by Doane R. Hoag). *Ph:* John Alton. *Ed:* James Leicester. *Mus:* Louis Forbes. *With* Teresa Wright (*Ellen Braden*), Macdonald Carey (*Douglas Madison*), Dolores Moran (*Paula Mitchener*), Adele Mara (*Gracie*), Edgar Barrier (*Gillespie*), John Craven (*George Braden*), Jack Elam (*Max Verne*), Ralph Sanford (*Alvin Taylor*). *Prod:* Benedict Bogeaus for RKO. 74m.

CHINA VENTURE (1953). Marines rescue wounded Japanese admiral who has vital information. *Sc:* George Worthing Yates, Richard Collins (from a story by Anson Bond). *Ph:* Sam Leavitt. *Art dir:* Edward Ilou. *Ed:* Jerome Thoms. *Mus:* Ross di Maggio. *With* Edmond O'Brien (*Capt. Matt Reardon*), Barry Sullivan (*Cmdr. Bert Thompson*), Jocelyn Brando (*Lt. Ellen Wilkins*), Leo Gordon (*Sgt. Hank Janowicz*), Richard Loo (*Chang Sung*), Dayton Lummis (*Dr. Masterson*), Leon Askin (*Wu King*), Dabbs Greer (*Galuppo*), Alvy Moore (*Carlson*), Philip Ahn (*Adm. Amara*), Wong Artarne (*Ensign Wong*), Guy Way (*Salomon*), Frank Wilcox (*Capt. Dryden*), James Anderson (*Corp. Walters*), Rex Reason (*Lt. Cross*), Todd Karns (*Lt. March*), Flame (*K-9 Corps Dog*). *Prod:* Anson Bond for Columbia. 80m.

RIOT IN CELL BLOCK 11 (1954). Convicts take over prison to demonstrate demands for better conditions. *Sc:* Richard Collins. *Ph:* Russell Harlan. *Art dir:* David Milton. *Ed:* Bruce Pierce. *Mus:* Herschel Burke Gilbert. *With* Neville Brand (*Dunn*), Emile Meyer (*The Warden*), Frank Faylen (*Haskel*), Leo Gordon (*Carnie*), Paul Frees (*Monroe*), Don Keefer (*Newspaperman*), Alvy Moore (*Gator*), Dabbs Greer (*Schuyler*), Whit Bissell (*Snader*), James Anderson (*Acton*), Carleton Young (*Capt. Barrett*), Harold J. Kennedy (*Graphic Reporter*), William Schallert (*1st Reporter*), Jonathan Hale (*Russell*), Robert Patten (*Frank*), William Phipps (*Mickey*), Joel Fluellen (*Al*), Roy Glenn (*Delmar*), Joe Kerr (*Mac*), John Tarangelo (*Manuel*), Robert Burton (*Ambrose*). *Prod:* Walter Wanger for Allied Artists. 80m.

PRIVATE HELL 36 (1954). Detectives lift part of recovered cache of money, leading to one's death. *Sc:* Collier Young, Ida Lupino. *Ph:* Burnett Guffey. *Art dir:* Walter Keller. *Ed:* Stanford Tischler. *Mus:* Leith Stevens. *With* Ida Lupino (*Lilli Marlowe*), Steve Cochran (*Cal*

193

Bruner), Howard Duff (*Jack Farnham*), Dean Jagger (*Capt. Michaels*), Dorothy Malone (*Francey Farnham*), Bridget Duff (*Farnham's Child*), Jerry Hausner (*Night Club Boss*), Dabbs Greer (*Bartender*), Chris O'Brien (*Coroner*), Kenneth Patterson (*Superior Officer*), George Dockstader (*Fugitive*), Jimmy Hawkins (*Delivery Boy*), King Donovan (*Burglar*). *Prod:* Collier Young for The Filmakers. 80m.

AN ANNAPOLIS STORY (GB: THE BLUE AND THE GOLD) (1955). Naval academy is site of romantic clash between brothers over one's girl. *Sc:* Dan Ullman, Geoffrey Homes [Daniel Mainwaring] (from a story by Dan Ullman). *Ph:* Sam Leavitt. *Ed:* William Austin. *Mus:* Martin Skiles. *With* John Derek (*Tony Scott*), Diana Lynn (*Peggy Lord*), Kevin McCarthy (*Jim Scott*), Alvy Moore (*Willie*), Pat Conway (*Dooley*), L. Q. Jones (*Watson*), John Kirby (*Macklin*), Barbara Brown (*Mrs. Scott*), Betty Lou Gerson (*Mrs. Lord*), Fran Bennett (*Connie*), Robert Osterloh (*Austin*), John Doucette (*Boxing Coach*), Don Haggerty (*Prentiss*). *Prod:* Walter Mirisch for Allied Artists. 87m. Technicolor.

INVASION OF THE BODY SNATCHERS (1956). Battle of last hold-outs against transformation into emotionless "pods". *Sc:* Daniel Mainwaring (from story "The Body Snatchers" by Jack Finney). *Ph:* Ellsworth Fredericks. *Art dir:* Ted Haworth. *Ed:* Robert S. Eisen. *Mus:* Carmen Dragon. *With* Kevin McCarthy (*Dr. Miles Bennell*), Dana Wynter (*Becky Driscoll*), Larry Gates (*Dr. Danny Kauffman*), King Donovan (*Jack Belicec*), Carolyn Jones (*Teddy Belicec*), Jean Willes (*Sally*), Ralph Dumke

(*Nick*), Virginia Christine (*Wilma*), Tom Fadden (*Uncle Ira*), Kenneth Patterson (*Mr. Driscoll*), Guy Way (*Sam Jansen*), Eileen Stevens (*Mrs. Grimaldi*), Beatrice Maude (*Grandma*), Jean Andren (*Aunt Eleda*), Bobby Clark (*Jimmy Grimaldi*), Everett Glass (*Dr. Percy*), Dabbs Greer (*Mac—Gas Station Prop.*), Pat O'Malley (*Baggage Man*), Guy Rennie (*Restaurant Proprietor*), Marie Selland (*Martha*), Whit Bissell (*Dr. Hill*), Richard Deacon (*Dr. Bassett*), Sam Peckinpah (*Gas Meter Reader*). *Prod:* Walter Wanger for Allied Artists. 80m. SuperScope.

CRIME IN THE STREETS (1956). Slum gang plans murder of neighbour, foiled by understanding social worker. *Sc:* Reginald Rose. *Ph:* Sam Leavitt. *Art dir:* Serge Krizman. *Ed:* Richard C. Meyer. *Mus:* Franz Waxman. *With* James Whitmore (*Ben Wagner*), John Cassavetes (*Frankie Dane*), Sal Mineo (*Baby Gioia*), Mark Rydell (*Lou Macklin*), Virginia Gregg (*Mrs. Dane*), Peter Votrian (*Richie Dane*), Will Kuluva (*Mr. Gioia*), Malcolm Atterbury (*Mr. McAllister*), Denise Alexander (*Maria Gioia*), Dan Terranova (*Blockbuster*), Peter Miller, Steve Rowland, Ray Stricklyn, James Ogg, Robert Alexander, Duke Mitchell, Richard Curtis, Doyle Baker. *Prod:* Vincent M. Fennelly for Allied Artists. 91m.

SPANISH AFFAIR (1957). Glossy romance in Spanish setting of architect and beautiful translator. *Sc:* Richard Collins. *Ph:* Sam Leavitt. *Art dirs:* Hal Pereira and Tambi Larsen. *Ed:* Tom McAdoo. *Mus:* Daniele Amfitheatrof. *With* Richard Kiley (*Merritt Blake*), Carmen Sevilla (*Mari Zarubia*), Jose Guardiola (*Antonio*), Jesus Tordesillas (*Sotelo*), Jose Marco Davo (*Father*), Jose Manuel Martin (*Fernan-*

do), Francisco Bernal (*Waiter*), Purita Vargas (*Purita*), Antonio S. Amaya (*Miguel*), Rafael Farina (*Flamenco Singer*). *Prod:* Bruce Odlum for Paramount. 93m. Technicolor. VistaVision.

BABY FACE NELSON (1957). Prohibition/Depression Mid-West is scene of violent robberies led by psycho killer. *Sc:* Irving Shulman, Daniel Mainwaring (story by Robert Adler). *Ph:* Hal Mohr. *Ed:* Leon Barsha. *With* Mickey Rooney (*Nelson*), Carolyn Jones (*Sue*), Sir Cedric Hardwicke (*Doc Saunders*), Chris Dark (*Jerry*), Ted de Corsia (*Rocca*), Emile Meyer (*Mac*), Tony Caruso (*Hamilton*), Leo Gordon (*Dillinger*), Dan Terranova (*Miller*), Jack Elam (*Fatso*), Dabbs Greer (*Bonner*), Robert Osterloh (*Johnson*), Dick Crockett (*Powell*), Paul Baxley (*Aldridge*), Thayer David (*Connelly*), Ken Patterson (*Vickman*), Sol Gorse (*Preston*), Gil Perkins (*Duncan*), Tom Fadden (*Harkins*), Lisa Davis (*Ann Saper, the lady in red*), John Hoyt (*Parker*), Elisha Cook Jr. (*Van Meter*), Murray Alper (*Bank Guard*), George Stone (*Mr. Hall*), Hubie Kerns (*Kearns*), Paul and Richard Donnelly (*the two boys*). *Prod:* Al Zimbalist for United Artists. 85m.

THE GUN RUNNERS (1958). Hard-up sailor uses boat to run guns to Cuba for crook. *Sc:* Daniel Mainwaring, Paul Monash (from "To Have and Have Not" by Ernest Hemingway). *Ph:* Hal Mohr. *Art dir:* Howard Richmond. *Ed:* Chester Schaeffer. *Mus:* Leith Stevens. *With* Audie Murphy (*Sam Martin*), Eddie Albert (*Hanagan*), Patricia Owens (*Lucy Martin*), Everett Sloane (*Harvey*), Gita Hall (*Eva*), Richard Jaeckel (*Buzurki*), Paul Birch (*Sy Phillips*), Jack Elam (*Arnold*),

John Harding (*Peterson*), Peggy Maley (*Blondie*), Carlos Romero (*Carlos*), Edward Colmans (*Juan*), Steven Peck (*Pepito*), Lita Leon (*Pepita*), Ted Jacques (*Commander Walsh*), John Qualen (*Pop*), Freddie Roberto (*Berenguer*). *Prod:* Clarence Greene for United Artists. 83m.

THE LINE-UP (1958). Hoodlums pursue drug cache through San Francisco in race against time and capture by police. *Sc:* Stirling Silliphant (based on CBS television series, created by Lawrnce L. Klee). *Ph:* Hal Mohr. *Art dir:* Ross Bellah. *Ed:* Al Clark. *With* Eli Wallach (*Dancer*), Robert Keith (*Julian*), Warner Anderson (*Lt. Guthrie*), Richard Jaeckel (*Sandy McLain*), Mary La Roche (*Dorothy Bradshaw*), William Leslie (*Larry Warner*), Emile Meyer (*Insp. Al Quine*), Marshall Reed (*Insp. Fred Asher*), Raymond Bailey (*Philip Dressler*), Vaughn

Cornel Wilde with Mickey Shaughnessy in EDGE OF ETERNITY

195

Taylor (*The Man*), Cheryl Callaway (*Cindy*), Bert Holland (*Porter No. 1*), George Eldredge (*Dr. Turkel*), Robert Bailey (*Staples*). *Prod:* Jaime Del Valle for Columbia. 86m.

EDGE OF ETERNITY (1959). Gold mine deaths investigated by Deputy Sheriff near Grand Canyon. *Sc:* Knut Swenson, Richard Collins (from a story by Ben Markson and Knut Swenson). *Ph:* Burnett Guffey. *Art dir:* Robert Peterson. *Ed:* Jerome Thoms. *Mus:* Daniele Amfitheatrof. *With* Cornel Wilde (*Les Martin*), Victoria Shaw (*Janice Kendon*), Mickey Shaughnessy (*Scotty O'Brien*), Edgar Buchanan (*Sheriff Edwards*), Rian Garrick (*Bob Kendon*), Jack Elam (*Bill Ward*), Alexander Lockwood (*Jim Kendon*), Dabbs Greer (*Gas Station Attendant*), Tom Fadden (*Eli*), Wendell Holmes (*Sam Houghton*), George Cisar (*The Dealer*), Buzz Westcott (*Pilot*), Ted Jacques (*Suds Reese*), Paul Bailey (*Amphibian Pilot*), Don Siegel (*Man at the pool*). *Prod:* Kendrick Sweet for Columbia. 80m. **Eastmancolor. Cinema-Scope.**

HOUND DOG MAN (1959). Boy and dog taken on hunting trip by older brother and friend. *Sc:* Fred Gipson, Winston Miller (from a novel by Fred Gipson). *Ph:* Charles G. Clarke. *Art dirs:* Lyle R. Wheeler, Walter M. Simonds. *Ed:* Louis Loeffler. *Mus:* Cyril Mockridge. *With* Fabian (*Clint*), Carol Lynley (*Dony*), Stuart Whitman (*Blackie Scantling*), Arthur O'Connell (*Aaron McKinney*), Dodie Stevens (*Nita Stringer*), Betty Field (*Cora*), Royal Dano (*Fiddling Tom Waller*), Margo Moore (*Susie Bell*), Claude Akins (*Hog Peyson*), Edgar Buchanan (*Doc Cole*), Jane Darwell

(*Grandma Wilson*), L. Q. Jones (*Dave Wilson*), Virginia Gregg (*Amy Waller*), Dennis Holmes (*Spud McKinney*), Rachel Stephens (**Rachel Wilson**), Jim Beck (**Terminus Dooley**), Hope Summers (*Jewell Crouch*), Harry Carter (*Sol Fikes*). *Prod:* Jerry Wald for Twentieth Century-Fox. 87m. Colour by DeLuxe. CinemaScope.

FLAMING STAR (1960). Mixed family nearly exterminated in war between Indians and whites. *Sc:* Clair Huffaker, Nunnally Johnson (from a novel by Clair Huffaker). *Ph:* Charles G. Clarke. *Art dirs:* Duncan Cramer, Walter M. Simonds. *Ed:* Hugh S. Fowler. *Mus:* Cyril Mockridge. *With* Elvis Presley (*Pacer Burton*), Steve Forrest (*Clint Burton*), Barbara Eden (*Roslyn Pierce*), Dolores Del Rio (*Neddy Burton*), John McIntire (*Pa Burton*), Rudolfo Acosta (*Buffalo Horn*), Karl Swenson (*Dred Pierce*), Ford Rainey (*Doc Phillips*), Richard Jaeckel (*Angus Pierce*), Anne Benton (*Dorothy Howard*), Douglas Dick (*Will Howard*), L. Q. Jones (*Tom Howard*), Tom Reese (*Jute*), Marian Goldina (*Shaknay*), Monty Burkhart (*Ben Ford*), Ted Jacques (*Horsby*), Rodd Redwing (*Indian brave*), Perry Lopez (*Two Moons*), Tom Fadden (*Townsman*). *Prod:* David Weisbart for Twentieth Century-Fox. 101m. Colour by DeLuxe. CinemaScope.

HELL IS FOR HEROES (1962). Misfit takes command of unit near Siegfried Line in Second World War. *Sc:* Robert Pirosh, Richard Carr (from a story by Robert Pirosh). *Ph:* Harold Lipstein. *Ed:* Howard Smith. *Mus:* Leonard Rosenman. *With* Steve McQueen (*Reese*), Bobby Darin (*Corby*), Fess Parker (*Sgt. Pike*), Nick Adams (*Homer*), Bob Newhart

HOUND DOG MAN: Claude Akins, Margo Moore, Fabian, and Carol Lynley

(*Driscoll*), Harry Guardino (*Sgt. Larkin*), James Coburn (*Henshaw*), Mike Kellin (*Kolinski*), Joseph Hoover (*Capt. Loomis*), Bill Mullikin (*Cumberly*), L. Q. Jones (*Sgt. Frazer*), Michele Montan (*Monique*), Don Haggerty (*Captain*). Prod: Henry Blanke for Paramount. 89m.

THE KILLERS (1964). Professionals gun ex-auto racer, unravel million dollar mail robbery. Sc: Gene L. Coon (from the short story by Ernest Hemingway). Ph: Richard L. Rawlings. Art dirs: Frank Arrigo, George Chan. Ed: Richard Belding. Mus: Johnny Williams. With Lee Marvin (*Charlie Strom*), John Cassavetes (*Johnny North*), Angie Dickinson (*Sheila Farr*), Ronald Reagan (*Browning*), Clu Gulager (*Lee*), Claude Akins (*Earl Sylvester*), Norman Fell (*Mickey*), Virginia Christine (*Miss Watson*), Don Haggerty (*Mail Truck Driver*), Robert Phillips (*George*), Kathleen O'Malley (*Receptionist*), Ted Jacques (*Gym Assistant*), Irving Mosley (*Mail Truck Guard*), Jimmy Joyce (*Salesman*), Scott Hale (*Desk Clerk*), Seymour Cassel (*2nd Clerk*). Prod: Don Siegel for Universal. 95m. Colour by Pathe. Panavision.

THE HANGED MAN (1964). Crooked union official blackmailed by friend of presumed victim. *Sc:* Jack Laird, Stanford Whitmore (from a novel by Dorothy Hughes). *Ph:* Bud Thackery. *Art dir:* John J. Lloyd. *Ed:* Richard Belding. *With* Robert Culp (*Harry Pace*), Edmond O'Brien (*Arnie Seeger*), Vera Miles (*Lois Seeger*), Norman Fell (*Gaylord Greb*), Gene Raymond (*Whitey Devlin*), Brenda Scott (*Çeline*), J. Carroll Naish (*Uncle Picaud*), Pat Buttram (*Otis Honeywell*), Edgar Bergen (*Hotel Clerk*), Archie Moore (*Xavier*), Randy Boone (*Boy*), Seymour Cassel (*Bellboy*), Scott Hale (*TV Newsman*), Al Lettieri, Astrid Gilberto, Stan Getz. *Prod:* Ray Wagner for Universal. 96m. Technicolor. Panavision.

STRANGER ON THE RUN (1967). Fonda, as drifter wrongly accused of murder by hostile railroad sheriff Parks, sent on chase through desert, helped by courageous widow Baxter. *Sc:* Dean Riesner (from a story by Reginald Rose). *Ph:* Bud Thackery. *Art dir:* W. D. Decives. *Ed:* Richard Wray. *Mus:* Stanley Wilson. *With* Henry Fonda (*Ben Chamberlain*), Anne Baxter (*Valverda Johnson*), Dan Duryea (*O. E. Hotchkiss*), Michael Parks (*Vince McKay*), Sal Mineo (*Blaylock*), Tom Reese (*Leo Weed*), Michael Burns (*Matt Johnson*), Lloyd Bochner (*Gorman*), Madlyn Rhue (*Alma Britten*), Bernie Hamilton (*Dickory*), and Zalman King. *Prod:* Richard E. Lyons for Universal. 97m. Technicolor. Panavision.

MADIGAN (1968). Two detectives have seventy-two hours to catch escaped killer. *Sc:* Henri Simoun [Howard Rodman], Abraham Polonsky (based on the novel "The Commissioner" by Richard Dough-

erty). *Ph:* Russell Metty. *Art dirs:* Alexander Golitzen, George C. Webb. *Ed:* Milton Shifman. *Mus:* Don Costa. *With* Richard Widmark (*Dan Madigan*), Henry Fonda (*Commissioner Anthony X. Russell*), Inger Stevens (*Julia Madigan*), Harry Guardino (*Rocco Bonaro*), James Whitmore (*Chief Insp. Charles Kane*). Susan Clark (*Tricia Bentley*), Michael Dunn (*Midget Castiglione*), Steve Ihnat (*Barney Benesch*), Don Stroud (*Hughie*), Sheree North (*Jonesy*), Warren Stevens (*Ben Williams*), Raymond St. Jacques (*Dr. Taylor*), Bert Freed (*Chief of Det. Hap Lynch*), Harry Bellaver (*Mickey Dunn*), Frank Marth (*Lt. James Price*), Lloyd Gough (*Earl Griffen*), Virginia Gregg (*Esther Newman*), Henry Beckman (*Ptl. Philip Downes*), Woodrow Parfrey (*Marvin*), Dallas Mitchell (*Det. Tom Gavin*), Lloyd Haines (*Ptl. Sam Woodley*), Ray Montgomery (*Det. O'Mara*), Seth Allen (*Subway Dispatcher*), Kay Turner (*Stella*), Scott Hale (*Ambulance Driver*). *Prod:* Frank P. Rosenberg for Universal. 101m. Technicolor. TechniScope.

COOGAN'S BLUFF (1969). Arizona lawman pursues maniacal criminal in Manhattan. *Sc:* Herman Miller, Dean Riesner, Howard Rodman (based on a story by Herman Miller). *Ph:* Bud Thackery. *Art dirs:* Alexander Golitzen, Robert C. MacKichan. *Ed:* Sam Waxman. *Mus:* Lalo Schifrin. *With* Clint Eastwood (*Coogan*), Lee J. Cobb (*Sheriff McElroy*), Susan Clark (*Julie*), Tisha Sterling (*Linny Raven*), Don Stroud (*Ringerman*), Betty Field (*Mrs. Ringerman*), Tom Tully (*Sheriff McCrea*), Melodie Johnson (*Millie*), James Edwards (*Jackson*), Rudy Diaz (*Running Bear*), David F.

Doyle (*Pushie*), Louis Zorich (*Taxi Driver*), Meg Myles (*Big Red*), Marjorie Bennett (*Mrs. Fowler*), Seymour Cassel (*Young Hood*), John Coe (*Bellboy*), Skip Battyn (*Omega*), Albert Popwell (*Wonderful Digby*), Conrad Bain (*Madison Ave. Man on helicopter*), James Gavin (*Ferguson*), Albert Henderson (*Desk Sergeant*), James McCallion (*Room Clerk*), Syl Lamont (*Manager*), Jess Osuna (*Prison Hospital Guard*), Jerry Summers (*Good Eyes*), Antonia Rey (*Mrs. Amador*), Marya Henriques (*Go-Go Dancer*). *Prod:* Don Siegel for Universal. 94m. Technicolor. Panavision.

DEATH OF A GUNFIGHTER (1969). Western marshal, rejected by townspeople because he knows too much, killed on day of wedding to town madam. *Sc:* James Calvelli (based on a novel by Lewis B. Patten). *Ph:* Andrew Jackson. *Mus:* Oliver Nelson. *With* Richard Widmark (*Marshal Frank Patch*), Lena Horne (*Claire Quintana*), Carroll O'Connor (*Lester Locke*), David Opatoshu (*Edward Rosenbloom*), Kent Smith (*Andrew Oxley*), Jacqueline Scott (*Laurie Mills*), Morgan Woodward (*Ivan Stanek*), Larry Gates (*Mayor Chester Sayre*), Dub Taylor (*Doc Adams*), John Saxon (*Lou Trinidad*), Darleen Carr (*Hilda Jorgenson*), Michael McGreevey (*Dan Joslin*), Royal Dano (*Arch Brandt*), James Lydon (*Luke Mills*), Kathleen Freeman (*Mary Elizabeth*), Harry Carey, Jr. (*Rev. Rork*), Amy Thomson (*Angela*), Mercer Harris (*Will Oxley*), James O'Hara (*Father Sweeney*), Walter Sande (*Paul Hammond*), Victor French (*Phil Miller*), Robert Sorrells (*Chris Hogg*), Charles Kuenstle (*Roy Brandt*), Sara Taft (*Mexican Woman*). *Prod:*

Richard E. Lyons for Universal. 94m. Technicolor.

TWO MULES FOR SISTER SARA (1970). Pro-Juarista nun and mercenary team up to vanquish French garrison; nun revealed as prostitute. *Sc:* Albert Maltz (from a story by Budd Boetticher). *Ph:* Gabriel Figueroa. *Art dir:* Jose Rodriguez Granada. *Ed:* Robert F. Shugrue. *Mus:* Ennio Morricone. *With* Shirley MacLaine (*Sara*), Clint Eastwood (*Hogan*), Manolo Fabregas (*Col. Beltran*), Alberto Morin (*Gen. LeClaire*), Armando Silvestre (*1st American*), John Kelly (*2nd American*), Enrique Lucero (*3rd American*), David Estuardo (*Juan*), Ada Carrasco (*Juan's Mother*), Poncho Cordoba (*Juan's Father*), Jose Chavez (*Horacio*), Pedro Galvan, Jose Angel Espinosa, Aurora Munoz, Xavier Marc, Hortensia Santovena, Rosa Furman, Jose Torvay, Margarita Luna and Javier Masse. *Prod:* Martin Rackin for Universal. 105m. Technicolor. Panavision.

THE BEGUILED (1971). Union soldier, nursed in Southern girls' school, suffers amputation and death. *Sc:* John B. Sherry, Grimes Grice [Albert Maltz] (from a novel by Thomas Cullinan). *Ph:* Bruce Surtees. *Art dir:* Alexander Golitzen. *Ed:* Carl Pingitore. *Mus:* Lalo Schifrin. *With* Clint Eastwood (*John McBurney*), Geraldine Page (*Martha*), Elizabeth Hartman (*Edwina*), Jo Ann Harris (*Carol*), Darleen Carr (*Doris*), Mae Mercer (*Hallie*), Pamelyn Ferdin (*Amy*), Melody Thomas (*Abigail*), Peggy Drier (*Lizzie*), Pattye Mattick (*Janie*). *Prod:* Don Siegel for Universal. 105m. Technicolor. Panavision.

DIRTY HARRY (1971). Cop tracks "Scorpio" killer over roofs, through streets

199

of San Francisco, then finally on school bus with terrified children. *Sc:* Harry Julian Fink, R. M. Fink, Dean Riesner (from a story by Harry Julian Fink and R. M. Fink). *Ph:* Bruce Surtees. *Art dir:* Dale Hennesy. *Ed:* Carl Pingitore. *Mus:* Lalo Schifrin. *With* Clint Eastwood (*Harry*), Harry Guardino (*Bressler*), Reni Santoni (*Chico*), Andy Robinson (*Killer*), John Larch (*Chief*), John Mitchum (*DeGeorgio*), Mae Mercer (*Mrs. Russell*), Lyn Edgington (*Norma*), Ruth Kobart (*Bus Driver*), Woodrow Parfrey (*Mr. Jaffe*), Josef Sommer (*Rothko*), William Paterson (*Bannerman*), James Nolan (*Liquor Proprietor*), Maurice S. Argent (*Sid Kleinman*), Jo De Winter (*Miss Willis*), Craig G. Kelly (*Sgt. Reineke*), John Vernon (*The Mayor*). *Prod:* Don Siegel for Warner Bros. 102m. Technicolor, Panavision.

CHARLEY VARRICK (1973). Nevada crop duster turns to bank robbery, accidentally grabs Mafia money, eludes pursuers. *Sc:* Dean Riesner, Howard Rodman (from the novel "The Looters" by John Reese). *Ph:* Michael Butler. *Art dir:* Fernando Carrere. *Ed:* Frank Morriss. *Mus:* Lalo Schifrin. *With* Walter Matthau (*Charley Varrick*), Andy Robinson (*Harman Sullivan*), Joe Don Baker (*Molly*), John Vernon (*Maynard Boyle*), Felicia Farr (*Sybil Forte*), Sheree North (*Jewell Everett*), Norman Fell (*Damon Garfinkle*), Jacqueline Scott (*Nadine Varrick*), Tom Tully (*Tom, Gun Store Proprietor*), William Schallert (*Sheriff Bill Horton*), Woodrow Parfrey (*Howard Young*), Marjorie Bennett (*Mrs. Taff*), Colby Chester (*"Stainless" Steele*), Rudy

Diaz (*Sanchez*), Don Siegel (*Murph*). *Prod:* Don Siegel for Universal. 101m. Technicolor. Panavision.

THE BLACK WINDMILL (DRABBLE) (1974). Kidnapped son of agent Caine held for ransom of government-owned diamonds; double dealing and chases through London and Paris end at Sussex windmill. *Sc:* Leigh Vance (from novel "Ten Days To a Killing" by Clive Egleton). *Ph:* Ousama Rawi. *Art dir:* Peter Murton. *Ed:* Antony Gibbs. *Mus:* Roy Budd. *With* Michael Caine (*Maj. John Tarrant*), Donald Pleasence (*Cedric Harper*), Janet Suzman (*Alex Tarrant*), Delphine Seyrig (*Ceil Burrows*), Clive Revill (*Alf Chestermann*), John Vernon (*McKee*), Joss Ackland (*Supt. Wray*), Joseph O'Conor (*Sir Edward Julyan*), Catherine Schell (*Melissa Julyan*), Hermione Baddeley (*Hetty*), Denis Quilley (*Bateson*), Edward Hardwicke (*Mike McCarthy*), Joyce Carey (*Miss Monley, Harper's Sec'y*), Paul Moss (*David Tarrant*), Mark Praid (*James Stroud*), Preston Lockwood (*Ilkeston, Bank Mgr.*), Robert Dorning (*Jeweller*), Yves Afonso (*Jacques*), David Daker, Patrick Barr, John Rhys Davies. *Prod:* Don Siegel for Universal. *Assoc. prod:* Scott Hale. 106m. Technicolor. Panavision.

MONTAGE Siegel did the montage sequences for many Warner Bros. features from about 1935 to 1944 including *The Roaring Twenties* (1939), *The Santa Fe Trail* (1940), *They Died with their Boots On* (1942), and *Blues in the Night* (1941). Siegel's name appears on the credits as montage director (with James Leicester) of: *Yankee Doodle Dandy*

Opposite: Don Siegel on CHARLEY VARRICK

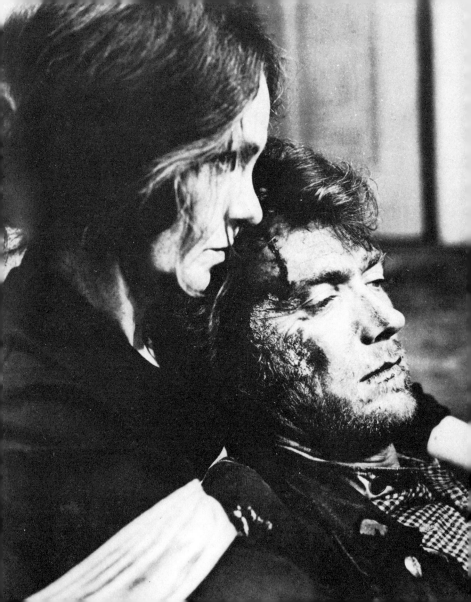

(1942), *Mission to Moscow* (1943), *Casablanca* (1943), and *Adventures of Mark Twain* (1944). Also on *Confessions of a Nazi Spy* (1939), *Knute Rockne, All American* (1940), *Gentleman Jim* (1942), *Background to Danger* (1943), and *Edge of Darkness* (1943).

SECOND UNIT Siegel served as second unit director on about 40 Warner Bros.

features of the period including: Howard Hawks' *Sergeant York* (1941), Raoul Walsh's *Northern Pursuit* (1943), Michael Curtiz' *Passage to Marseilles* (1944), and Sam Wood's *Saratoga Trunk* (1945). Siegel also directed, without credit by his own choosing, the second unit for Robert Rossen's film *All the King's Men* (1949) at Columbia.

This book is dedicated to Don Siegel and Ceil Burrows.

Acknowledgements (Siegel)

Gene Giaquinto, Universal; Joseph Goldberg, PhD.; Milt Kass; Donald Krim, United Artists; Peter Meyer; Gary Roselman, Avcom Motion Picture Supply, New York; Charles Silver, Museum of Modern Art; Elliott Stein; Pat White; Jacobo Brender; Elio Mujica.

Opposite: Geraldine Page and Clint Eastwood in THE BEGUILED.

Index to Names in Text